FISHERMAN'S BLUES

FISHERMAN'S BLUES

A West African Community at Sea

▽ ▲ ▽

ANNA BADKHEN

RIVERHEAD BOOKS
New York
2018

RIVERHEAD BOOKS
An imprint of Penguin Random House LLC
375 Hudson Street
New York, New York 10014

Copyright © 2018 by Anna Badkhen
Illustration on p. 55 by Ndongo Souaré, used by permission.
All other illustrations copyright © 2018 by Anna Badkhen

Library of Congress Cataloging-in-Publication Data

Names: Badkhen, Anna, 1975– author.
Title: Fisherman's blues : a West African community at sea / Anna Badkhen.
Description: New York : Riverhead Books, 2018.
Identifiers: LCCN 2017030225 (print) | LCCN 2017043065 (ebook) |
ISBN 9780698410848 (eBook) | ISBN 9781594634864 (hardback)
Subjects: LCSH: Fishing villages—Senegal—Joal-Fadiout. | Fishers—Senegal—Joal-Fadiout. |
Joal-Fadiout (Senegal)—Social life and customs. | Joal-Fadiout (Senegal)—Social conditions. |
Joal-Fadiout (Senegal)—Economic conditions. | BISAC: SOCIAL SCIENCE / Anthropology /
Cultural. | TRAVEL / Africa / West. | NATURE / Ecosystems & Habitats / Oceans & Seas.
Classification: LCC GT5904.5.S38 (ebook) | LCC GT5904.5.S38
B33 2018 (print) | DDC 307.76/2—dc23
LC record available at https://lccn.loc.gov/2017030225
p.   cm.

Printed in the United States of America
1   3   5   7   9   10   8   6   4   2

BOOK DESIGN BY MEIGHAN CAVANAUGH

*Penguin is committed to publishing works of quality and integrity.
In that spirit, we are proud to offer this book to our readers; however,
the story, the experiences, and the words are the author's alone.*

Nio far. (We're all in it together.)

—WOLOF PROVERB

The tide lifts these words, rocks them for a moment,
and then, with a swipe, erases them.

—OCTAVIO PAZ, "TARGET PRACTICE"

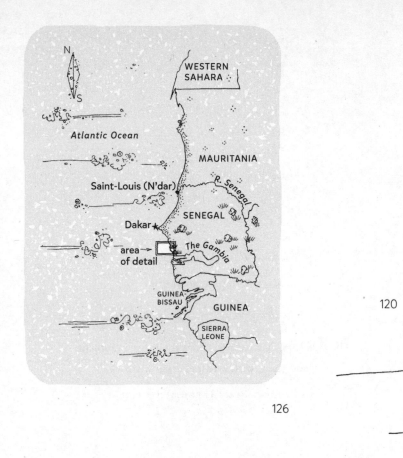

N
S

WESTERN
SAHARA

Atlantic Ocean

MAURITANIA

R. Senegal

Saint-Louis (N'dar)

SENEGAL

Dakar ★

area →
of detail

The Gambia

GUINEA-
BISSAU

GUINEA

SIERRA
LEONE

78

120

126

96

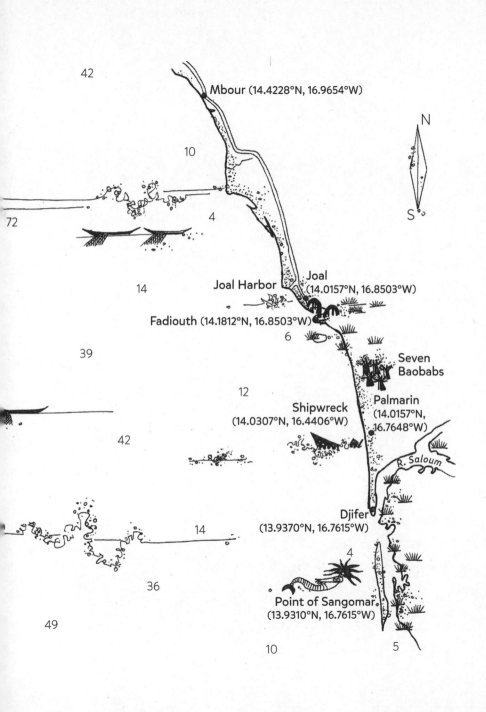

42

10

72

4

Mbour (14.4228°N, 16.9654°W)

N

S

Joal
(14.0157°N, 16.8503°W)

Joal Harbor

14

Fadiouth (14.1812°N, 16.8503°W)

6

39

Seven
Baobabs

12

Shipwreck
(14.0307°N, 16.4406°W)

Palmarin
(14.0157°N,
16.7648°W)

42

R. Saloum

Djifer
(13.9370°N, 16.7615°W)

14

4

36

Point of Sangomar
(13.9310°N, 16.7615°W)

49

10

5

FISHERMAN'S BLUES

One

End of the rainy season, high tide, a viscous black predawn. The Milky Way bulges, drips stars. Mahogany keels of fishing pirogues grate against the sucking purl. In the wrack before the moored thirty-footer the *Sakhari Souaré* her groggy crew stand barefoot in silence. It is not time yet.

A light approaches along the tideline, winks, grows. A fishwife. Her pace is measured, her slack arms swing lightly with her step, her back is very straight. She is wearing a mermaid dress. On her head flames a colossal brazier. She does not slow down when she reaches the fishers, and she passes them without greeting and walks away until she flickers out into the sweaty black.

▽ ▲ ▽

Dawn spills astern: lavender, violet, golden. Capillary waves gently scale the ocean all the way to the horizon. Wind clots low fog. The *Sakhari Souaré* glides at full throttle west-southwest, rolls over lazy six-foot swells. The shore's low skyline of baobab and eucalyptus and doum palms flashes in the light, sinks into the sea. Its bruised cumulus vanishes, too. Black against the banded east a seabird, an early riser, falls out of the fog and scoops something out of the water and banks away. The pirogue's six crew balance spreadlegged on the thwarts and on the foredeck, dig their bare soles into the slippery wood, lean into one another, watch the sea for fish.

A school of fish is an indentation in the surface, an irregularity in the wave pattern, a boil of bubbles you can see even in the blowing water of a gale. When a school rises, a patch of the sea stirs, jiggles, churns. Or it can be a hue: a denser ovoid sea, a shifting silver nebula. A kind of anticipatory shimmering, like something about to be born. You hold your breath for it.

When you spot a school of fish you signal with your hand. This is for the helmsman, usually the captain, who cannot hear over the droning outboard motor from his place in the stern. Right arm flies up: fish to starboard. Left arm: fish to port. An outstretched hand, loose wrist, fingers wave: bubbles. An outstretched hand, a jerking upturned palm, fingertips kiss and open, kiss and open: fish are jumping. The sign language is contagious. Come aboard and within hours your arms rise and your fingers wiggle as if by reflex. Maybe it is a reflex, one landdwellers have learned to suppress.

When you see no fish you keep your hands occupied or tucked away, lest you confuse the helmsman. He watches the dance of hands, adjusts the pirogue's course to the flutter of the crew's fingers. Adjusts his expectations. Thumb to the forefinger's first knuckle: fish too small, don't bother.

Genii herd the fish. Before coming aboard you try to divert their attention. This takes magic because genii remember backward: never the past, always the future. So you utter a prayer. You score kabbalistic shapes into the sand where it meets the sea. You pay a marabout or a sorcerer to pacify the genii on your behalf, to ask the sea for specific fish that sell well at the harbor: white grouper, say, or shadefish. The pricier the fish, the more elaborate the ritual to distract the genii that herd it. But in recent years, even fishers who go to sea for ordinary sardinella have been offering sacrifices to the genii, and even their sacrifices more often than not fail to secure a catch. Entire trips go by during which the captain stares at the limp arms of his crew. The sea is broken, fishermen say. The sea is empty. The genii have taken the fish elsewhere.

There is another explanation for the diminishing catch. It holds that man has meddled with the ocean's temperature, that increased salinity and chaotic weather patterns disrupt habitats, scare schools away. It holds, too, that man has decimated the fish stocks: along the three hundred and thirty miles of Senegal's coastline, twenty thousand pirogues like the *Sakhari Souaré* and dozens of foreign mechanized trawlers are wasting the fishery recklessly and daily.

Fishermen also say that they heard from their grandfathers who heard from their own grandfathers that the sea and the fish in it move through cycles that are far longer than the lunar months that chart the annual patterns of wind and waves and underwater migration—and, because the scope of their periodicity exceeds the memory of any man alive at any given time, are unknowable.

All these explanations are true, fishermen say, because the ocean has not one surface but multitudes, and each contains myriad realities that change all the time, delivering silver heaps of fish or combing the nets empty, recasting its own liminality infinitely, in an infinity of limitless iterations.

The *Sakhari Souaré* pilots these shifting tides. She is thirty feet long with a three-foot beam, very narrow at the hip. She has seven holds, six thwarts, no belowdecks, no deck. She is six years old and runs on a fifteen-horsepower twostroke outboard Yamaha motor that one of her crew hoists over his shoulder to take home each time she returns to port. She is flagged to Joal, Senegal's largest artisanal fishing port, a four-mile-long dune spit at the southern tip of the Petite Côte, just north of the fourteenth parallel. Her lifesaver is a car tire. She is a plank boat made shell-first on a keel of a single, scooped redwood trunk. That keel is a proto-pirogue, an echo of the Paleolithic canoes man the world over once gouged out of whole trees to go to sea.

Her hull below the waterline is brown, her gunwales are a scuffed red, her thwarts and ceiling once were white. Her topside is a psychedelic peacock's tail of green and yellow and red on a white field. Her nylon gillnet is half a mile long. Its sloppy accordion folds overflow the net hold, hover above it like froth. One end of the net lolls out, a gauzy pale green tongue that drapes the length of the boat just inside the port gunwale: this end will go in the water first. The net quivers in the westerly wind. Yellow styrofoam floats dangle from the swags. When you haul net hand over hand, you grab just below the floats and watch for fish in the mesh.

Now the pirogue stitches away from shore, a tiny wooden needle, her wake a fine embroidery on a surface that the morning sun has smoothed bluegreen and placid like blown glass. But the surface is depthless, an enormity of unknowns. It reflects the sky, just as enormous. It betrays nothing.

▽ ▲ ▽

By eight in the morning the westerlies pick up, chop the sea into a field of shards. The sky darkens and gains volume, billows, stretches. The pirogue takes the waves broadside, lolls, steadies, lolls again. The captain steers into the wind, into the swollen cloud.

The captain's name is Ndongo Souaré. He is thirty-seven years old, goateed, muscled, not tall. He sits in the stern, his knees wide apart, his left hand on the throttle. He is wearing a pair of newish secondhand bluejeans and a white nylon tee shirt with the neon logo of the national football team, the Lions of Teranga, and a baseball cap with the logo of a German trade union. The hat is frayed and faded to pink. He has draped his sweatshirt and a dark green fishing slicker across his chest diagonally, like a bandolier. All fishermen here do that. They follow an old fashion: in the creased sepia photographs the fishermen's grandfathers drape handwoven shawls or animal skins over their bare shoulders this way. The grandfathers never smile in the photographs. They level at the camera the same stare Captain Ndongo levels at the sea.

The *Sakhari Souaré* belongs to Ndongo's fisherman father, Amadou Souaré. She bears the name of his fisherman grandfather. Today her crew are all family: Ndongo, his sixteen-year-old nephew, two younger halfbrothers, and three sons.

The youngest on board is Ndongo's third-born, Maguette. He is an *oupa*: a decky, a tea boy, a fetcher of things, a roustabout. Every fishing pirogue has an *oupa,* sometimes two or three. An *oupa* is always the newest on the crew. Typically, the *oupas* are children. Watch them swim out to the boat to get the mooring line, then swim back pulling the vessel behind them closer to shore so that the older fishermen can wade aboard. Watch them strip naked and jump into the sea ten fathoms deep to scare fish into the net with their splashing. Watch them skip from thwart to gunwale to thwart—almost weightless, almost aflight, from stern to bow and back on fearless feet—balancing in their hands a cup of water or a po'boy with murex sauce or a lit cigarette for this mate or that, a hammer, a knife, a brazier with fuel-soaked coals for tea. The *oupa* is paid an equal share of the pirogue's catch, same as the first mate, same as the captain. As he grows he learns the ancient art of fishing. Ndongo was once an *oupa.*

Maguette on the forward thwart draws a chestful of air and

holds his breath behind puffed cheeks. Maybe he is waiting for fish. Maybe it's a game. A lot of what Maguette does is a game. He is twelve years old.

The boy holds and holds his breath until at last he loses his balance and nearly falls overboard. Ousmane, his eldest half-brother, catches him by the elbow, sucks his teeth in reprimand. Their father rebukes Maguette from the stern:

Eh! Stop acting like a kid.

The boy pulls a serious face, stretches, locks his hands at the nape of his neck. A faint low cloud draws over the sky, dull gray fog thickens, the sea calms, silvers in the shrouded sun, the texture of chinked glass.

A green sea turtle periscopes its head out of the water to starboard. The captain points, slows down the pirogue. Reconsiders, speeds up. It is illegal to catch turtles anymore, though men do.

Full throttle ahead again. Air flows past the pirogue in cold and warm layers. Farther to starboard terns drop into the water. A bumpy surface that way, a shiver. All aboard lift their right arms at once, fingers atwitch, and someone reaches for the net, but another gillnetter wheels across the bows, unfurling her own net behind her in a broad halo: she was here first. Ndongo stands up at the helm, raises his eyebrows, cups an upturned palm, shakes it side to side: What kind of fish?

Over the drone of the two outboards, a shouted response:

Rouget!

Okay, good luck!

Okay, God bless!

The *Sakhari Souaré* bears up. The other pirogue continues to circle, uncoils her net. For a time the two boats rotate away from each other on a tangent like cogs, helix the sea with the pearl strings of their dissolving wake. Below the surface the trapped fish are a fluid silver disc whirring in frenzied tapering loops. And above the fish and the sea and the boats the gray fogbank swirls upward to high cirrus smears, and for a moment the prey and the hunters and the sky form a vortex, a centripetal gyre of our becoming and undoing, a navel of the world.

⋎ ⋏ ⋎

Nine-forty A.M., ten miles south of Joal, six nautical miles offshore. High chop. The sea rocks the boat. Up and down, side to side: this is the rocking of the womb, the gentle swaying weightlessness that precedes our being, that our mothers prolong when they strap us to their backs in our first months, when they cradle us to sleep. But the rocking goes back further still, to that crepuscular beginning when we were microorganisms swished and tossed this way and that by the tide, a tide that has changed very little since, yet never stays the same.

Twelve million artisanal fishermen around the globe extend into adulthood this primal swaying, pass it on generation after generation. More than ten thousand of them call Joal their home port. For a season—a blink of the ocean's eye—I join this primordial sloshing. I go to sea aboard the *Sakhari Souaré*, aboard a

handful of other pirogues flagged to Joal. Gillnetters, purse seiners, trapsetters, jiggers.

After I come ashore the world continues to swing; it takes
hours to stop. *Mal de débarquement*, the disembarking sickness, a
neurological syndrome, a snag in the readaptation of the brain.
Typical symptoms: difficulty maintaining balance, persistent sen-
sation of swaying as the brain's response to the sudden physical
cessation of the waves' motion, to the sudden redundancy of sea
legs. The syndrome is little understood, may persist for years, and
lacks an effective treatment. I read somewhere that occurrence is
highest among women in their forties. I think it is a form of nos-
talgia. Most of us should be suffering from *mal de débarquement*.
Our land legs are brand-new.

To steady myself I look for something fixed, dependable. A
boundary of sorts. A line. But at sea the lines are multiple and
untrustworthy.

The impassive and unattainable horizon line, always receding,
asymptotic. Also besmirched: the line toward and beyond which,
for centuries, millions of men and women along this coast were
shackled and forced into slave ships.

The tideline, now receding to trap fishing boats in goop, now
advancing to lick entire villages off the shore, chronicling millennia of fluctuations: a dividing line, a line of fortification, a line of
defeat. "It is mainly the sea that gives the earth its outline and its
shape," wrote the ancient Greek historian Strabo. In truth, the
outline reshapes and reshapes. In the last twenty thousand years,
since the coldest part of the Ice Age, the shoreline has retreated

more than four hundred feet—and now is rising again, running along villages and towns like a tongue probing teeth.

The wrackline, ever revised, sketching out the littoral reaches and leavings of the ocean that gives so much yet withholds even more.

The fragile line between life and death at sea.

I look to my crewmates. They cross daily the inconstant boundary that divides our lives into the solid, the known, the terra firma—and the underexplored, the ephemeral, the everchanging. They are used to shaping a life on the elusive frontier between land and sea. But they know: this frontier is not binary; no boundary truly is. There is no real juxtaposition of the unfathomable and the solid. They stay afloat by keeping expectations fluid.

The ocean is the best opportunity God gave man. You can have fresh air and you can have fish.

Sometimes—sometimes—you can have fish. Today you get a lot of fish and tomorrow there is nothing. Impossible to predict.

It's a matter of chance.

In the sea, not knowing is part of being.

Life is so.

▽ ▲ ▽

Six or seven nautical miles offshore I bail the leaking *Sakhari Souaré* with a yellow plastic can that once held cooking oil. Her draft is four feet; to bail her you squat in the bilges and scoop and throw the rank water up and over, up and over, pause to watch the airborne spouts catch the sun. Above my head her gillnet sags into the holds, foams in the wind.

A gillnet hangs its sheer banner in the water and traps by the gills whatever runs into its mesh. It has a higher level of bycatch—the fish you didn't intend to haul—than a purse seine, which aims to scoop a specific school; in many parts of the world gillnetting is restricted or illegal. It is possible sometimes to squeeze the more slippery fish through the mesh intact, but generally you pick gillnet by ripping out the catch. Most things caught in it will die.

Gillnet, says Joal's oldest native fisherman, is the only net that you can use in Senegal to catch anything worthwhile.

A gillnetter is large enough to carry only one net, so you guess the diameter of the mesh to take onboard before you go to sea. Large fish will bounce off small-caliber mesh; small fish will slip through wide openings. Today Ndongo is casting a monofilament net with openings twenty-eight millimeters wide, four millimeters wider than the smallest caliber Senegal allows.

Ndongo steers broadside to the waves and a sea breaks over the port gunwale. The pirogue shakes; I bail harder; the boys on the thwarts adjust the bend of their knees to compensate for the sudden tilt, keep their eyes on the surface.

Cross-section the globe right here: the surface is also a line, a kinked cardiogram of the planet. Under the keel, in all that amniotic murk, do you see any fish?

⑦ ⚠ ⑦

W ind up to twenty knots blows the western sky full of
boiling black cloud, but overhead it has cleared and the
bright humid sun has swung to the south. In this light, aglow on
leaden seas, the pirogue is as if onstage. On her bow, the rusted
carcass of a shipwreck.

The skeletal frame of a cargo ship two hundred feet long. An
iron hull the color of dried blood the sea has whittled down to a
stalagmitic grid of sinew so filigreed it snapped in two amidships.
Her name misremembered, like her home port. Some say she was
hauling sugar from Banjul to Dakar when she ran aground a mile
or more offshore in 1978, the year Ndongo was born; her crew
deemed her unworthy of rescue and abandoned ship, and she
eventually drifted to her resting place within three hundred feet
of the low tidemark. Some say she was a Japanese boat carrying
electronics; her crew had brought her to the shore of the farming
village of Palmarin on purpose, to fix her engine, but discovered
that it was beyond saving, took the electronics, and journeyed on
by land. They say that no matter her history the villagers of Palmarin looted the ship, took everything they could, even the
walk-in freezers. The villagers laugh. Ridiculous! The village had
no electricity: What use would have been the freezers?

She tilts to port, pointing to shore, where between the green
shallows and the palm groves that give the village its name a row
of houses gape at the sea with their innards exposed, pink, blue,

ocher: the sea has taken their front walls. Macabre life-size doll-houses, their silence on display. Were there people inside them when the wave came, and did they survive the sea, and where are they now? Ndongo clicks his tongue in disapproval, says: Coastal erosion. All along the coast the ocean is sweeping the beach clean of homes. His own house, in Joal, is four thoughtful blocks in-land.

Grass grows on top of the poop deck. Water pours in and out of the disemboweled chambers with a slow *whoosh*, gurgles in the echoing cavities. In the labyrinths of the sunken hull, Ndongo says, fish hide.

Prepare to cast.

Ndongo issues orders quietly, almost inaudibly, safeguarding some hardwound coil of superstitious expectation. Or hiding his intentions from the genii below, as if the predatory contour of his boat is not giveaway enough.

The fishers pull on dark green rubberized overalls over ripped gym shorts. They pull on gloves knitted of skyblue polyester that unravel at the fingertips. They spread along the port gunwale and stand swaying over the net. Pirogues always cast to port. Who knows why? They have been doing so since time immemorial, in many disparate waters. Jesus's revolutionary advice to the luckless New Testament fishermen in the Sea of Galilee: "Cast your net to starboard."

Let go.

The crew bend as one and start ladling the net out to sea. Yard by nylon yard, arms straight, palms facing out, they push the mesh overboard in synchronous rapid motion. Coaxing it out. Offering it to the ocean as an oblation. Ndongo revs the engine and circles the shipwreck counterclockwise at an inward curl, and in the wake of the *Sakhari Souaré* the unspooling dotted yellow line of headrope floats draws a tightening conch around the rusted shell.

Faster, faster. Work like men, work like men.

The last of the net plashes into the water. The instant its fourfluked grapnel anchor slips out of the pirogue after it and sinks, the crew grab a hammer—a knife—an awl—a loose wooden burden board—and begin to whack the pirogue. They pummel the gunwales and the ceiling hard, and they stomp on the thwarts with bare feet in a ferocious and ancient abandon, and Ndongo heels the burden boards in the stern and pulses the accelerator. Amid this unholy sacrament the skinny boy Maguette swiftly strips down to cotton boxers and a red gris-gris belt weighed down with leather amulet pouches and somersaults into the spiral heart of the gillnet right by the shipwreck and there begins to splash madly in the green boil of the sea to scare the disoriented and deafened fish into his father's net.

Terrible clamor echoes off the corroded vaults. From roosts somewhere within the poop deck panicked pigeons fly out, scores of tumbling birds each piercingly defined in midmorning sun against the blueblack cloud. In the bow, the *Sakhari Souaré*'s first mate, one of Ndongo's halfbrothers, drops a board into the hold, reaches inside the waterproof pouch around his neck, pulls out a cellphone, turns his back to the wreck, and snaps a selfie.

Above the iron ossuary seabirds gather. Ndongo maneuvers the boat clockwise out of the maze of net, then steers her back into the spiral, cuts the motor, lifts it to run over the floatline, starts again. When he reaches the innermost end of the coil he cuts the motor again and motions to the crew: Haul net.

Like men now, like men.

They haul net hand over hand and lay it inside the boat in dripping crosswise pleats. They hum under their breath as they work, an old melody in a minor key, lonesome like the empty net they are hauling. It is ten o'clock.

Cast again.

Again the helical release, the mad whacking. On the bow the first mate again pulls out his cellphone. His name, too, is Maguette; he is twenty-four, Ndongo's halfbrother from their father's second wife. Ndongo named his son after him. He yells into the receiver:

Allo! Yes! Nothing yet! What you got? Okay! Okay, bye!

Who's that?

Baye Samb! He said he caught a full boat of mullet!

Do you want to call others and find out what they're catching?

Sure!

He squints at the screen, pushes buttons with a forefinger sticking out of a ripped blue glove.

Allo, it's me! No, no fish yet! Yes! You? Okay, if you find a lot of fish give us a call afterward, okay? Okay, godspeed!

The other fishers have spread out in the boat. Ousmane hauls the floatline, his uncle Saliou the leadline weighed down with handmolded slugs of lead and concrete, his cousin Ibrahima the middle. Hand over hand. Hand over hand.

The net snags.

Hey, Maguette, hang up and help!

They tug gently at the panel, lean so far out to port that the pirogue lists at forty-five degrees.

Careful, careful!

It's stuck on something underwater!

Quickly, quickly, we're losing time!

A yank, the net is loose, and bright brown seaweed sprays into the boat. They say in Japan men eat this stuff like salad.

Heave-ho.

They haul net. Ousmane, Ndongo's eldest surviving son, is fifteen; his firstborn died at birth—the first of three dead boys. Ousmane bears the brunt of the captain's parental hopes and disappointments; his lower lip is swollen and cracked, a pale crazing of scar and pustule from when he picks at it and chews it in stifled teenage recalcitrance. Saliou, Ndongo's other halfbrother, guesses he is nineteen. Ibrahima is sixteen, the eldest son of Ndongo's sister, and he is sporting a brand-new fancy footballer buzzcut, a flattop with a lightning bolt shaved above his left temple, and sings quietly, a hymn in approximated Arabic.

What are you singing, Ibrahima?

I dunno, something about Muhammad, peace be upon him.

Like men, like men. Work at the same speed so you haul at the same speed.

Ibrahima stops singing. The two Maguettes and Vieux, Ndon-

go's thirteen-year-old, sit on the starboard gunwale behind the
hauling crew, pick net.

A sompat grunt, about a foot long, spiny and speckled like a
hyena. A short-snouted cassava croaker. One—two—three juvenile threadfins no longer than three palms each. Small shiny flat
fish local fishermen call money of the sea. Villagers from inland
will sometimes buy those jerked. The boys toss them overboard—
there's plenty of good fish—and the fish sink past the confetti of
their own scales. Three or four recover and swim into the deep,
vanishing.

They throw the fish they choose to keep into the bilge amidships. Purple bruises from ruptured vessels spread along the dor-
sal fins and behind torn gills like ink on blotting paper. Ndongo
sucks his teeth again: disfigured fish will sell for less.

Watch it, watch how you pick, you're costing us money.

Little Maguette gathers in his fist a section of net where a pale

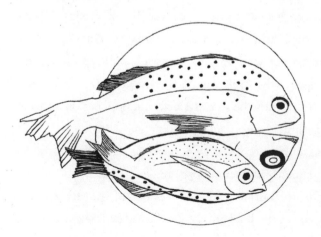

crab is stuck and smashes it against the gunwale again and again until the carapace breaks into bits small enough to shake out of the mesh. Crab entrails streak yellow and black on the kid's bright boxers with particolored cassette tape print. In the bilge a torn-off fish head dances on a single fin, flaps, flaps, stills.

Hurry up and haul. Keep the net level, it will make your work easier.

A rouget.

Okay, boys, hurry up, you're wasting time. Make this a quick one, we got places to be.

Ndongo admonishes in a low voice. At sea you must be careful to tone down your frustrations. Nothing on its endless surface to obstruct a disagreement from swelling into a brawl. Some of the waves that rock the *Sakhari Souaré* have traveled hundreds of miles across the Atlantic. The fetch length of grudges born here may be as oceanic, their toppling as deadly. In the Joal harbor returning fishers have tried to set one another's pirogues on fire.

In the bow Ousmane pries open the lid of a white plastic bucket that once held mayonnaise, rummages. An extra set of gloves, an awl, a screwdriver with a plastic handle painted in the stars and stripes of the American flag—here, a shuttle and a spool of fishline. He threads the shuttle slowly and perches on a thwart to mend a gash in the net.

Ousmane, hurry up, man, we're burning daylight. Ousmane. Did you hear me? I said get a move on!

The last of the outgoing tide sluices out of the shipwreck, a sucking sound. In the hold amidships the *Sakhari Souaré* a couple dozen fish are slowly dying in bloodied bilgewater. A severed head sloshes to and fro. Vieux, getting ready to bail, picks it up with two gloved fingers, tosses it overboard. The sea has flattened out again, bottlegreen against heavy sky. Suddenly the northern horizon vibrates, undulates, shatters: a pod of pelicans is flying low above the sea toward us. Ndongo sets course for the pelicans.

▽ ▲ ▽

I met Captain Ndongo Souaré the previous evening in Joal, in one of the seaside gazebos fishermen build to bide their time ashore. They call such gazebos *mbaars*.

Two thousand pirogues bristle the length of Joal; from the air, the town looks like a harlequin hedgehog stretched out alongside the Atlantic Ocean. There are no slips, no docks. The boats berth a wading distance offshore, anchored in the shallows, or right on the sandy beach, near one of the town's seventy-three mbaars.

Each *mbaar* reflects the affluence of the fishermen who use it. There are elaborate pavilions of poured concrete and corrugated tin roofs. There are improbable lean-tos cobbled together from bits of discarded pirogues stuck upright in the sand and roofed with the green meerschaum of tangled gillnet. Walls fashioned from tin, from rotten driftwood, from lacy curtains. Walls thatched with the droopy branches of filao, *Casuarina equisetifolia*, which French colonists imported to Senegal from Australia a few years before decolonization to contain erosion and fix nitrogen in the soil their own gluttonous hegemony had helped deplete. No walls at all. Lavish or poor, each *mbaar* is treated like a home: you take off your shoes before you enter, you clean up after yourself before you leave. Each bears the name of the fisherman who contributed the most to its construction or upkeep. Captain Coura Kane, a scion of one of Joal's oldest fishing families and the owner of several pirogues, paid the most to build the *mbaar* in which Ndongo hangs out; it is called Mbaar Kanené. It has nine beams of weathered tree trunks and a sloping tin roof. Its sole long bench is a board from a shipwrecked boat propped up on some broken concrete blocks. It has no walls. A jumble of nets, heaped in layers, takes up the whole floor; here men sit, mend nets, and talk fish. Here I came to find a skipper who would take me to sea.

For two decades, documenting the world's iniquities, I followed stories inland. I had never worked on the ocean. Now I wanted to learn: How does the shifting demarcation line between earth and sea define the way we see the world, shape our community and communality at the time of the Anthropocene? After my teenage son left for college, I ended my apartment lease in Philadelphia, stored my library in a friend's garage, gave away my furniture and warm clothes, and flew to Senegal.

It was late September, end of the rainy season. A hard rain blew, and a dozen regulars huddled in the center of the *mbaar*. Some sat, the others stood stretching, hands on the low roofbeams. Outside, on the sand, their boats were filling with rainwater: the *Cheikh Sadbou*, the *Fatou Fall*, the *Stacko Mbacké*, the *Khady*

Faye. Gillnetters mostly, named after the Prophet, the fishermen's wives, their favorite saints, their mothers and fathers and grandparents, because fishermen take their ancestors with them to sea. The rain made everything white. White sea blended into white sky. The pirogues lay at the edge of nothingness.

Hi.

A man squatted on a net a few feet away from me, out of the rain, his back to the sea.

Hi.

What's your name?

Anna.

Hi, Anna. I am Ndongo, Ndongo Souaré. Can I have one of your rings?

Rings are gris-gris. Like hair or blood, they hold the bearer's power. With the help of a sorcerer or a marabout, a new owner can use them to obtain some of that power, maybe even all of it. Rings are portals, too: a sorcerer can also manipulate them to inflict misfortune on the original owner. You burn or bury your hair and you burn or bury anything stained with your blood. You guard your jewelry. Nice try, Ndongo Souaré.

We have hardly met, I said. Maybe when we know each other a little better.

Before Ndongo could respond, a woman stormed in under the awning, and everyone in the *mbaar* turned to her. She was older, in a rich red dress and matching headwrap dripping with rainwater. Burgundy eyeliner traced stern lines over hairless brows.

Without stopping for *salaams* or to remove her flipflops, she made a beeline for the fisherman, gigantic in her rage. Ndongo shot to his feet.

You!

A manicured forefinger stabbed Ndongo's chest.

Where. Is. My. Shrimp. Have I not told you that I need shrimp? How come you sell your shrimp to the boys at the harbor when you know, tsk, you know by God!—she spat—that I need it myself. Thirty kilos. Eh? Eh? Useless. Useless!

The other fishermen bent to their nets in silence.

Yes, ma'am.

Well! Sorry, everyone.

A beautiful smile beneath those burgundy brows. Suddenly, a slight woman, short, in soggy red clothes, stood in the middle of the *mbaar*.

Salaam aleikum. How are you? How is the family? How is the work? How is the sea? Are you getting any fish?

Offered and returned, the salutations went round in the practiced millennial rhythm, an invocation of peace, your wife, your husband, your children, your work, your fish. She turned to me.

I am Fatou Diop Diagne, this one's mother.

A mother, a grandmother, a first wife, a co-wife. A fishwife, a midwife, a beignet maker, a hair braider, an embroiderer, a breakfast saleswoman. The keeper and assuager of the family's protector genie. The granddaughter of Lebou fishermen from Senegal's capital, Dakar. Whose own mother piloted fishing pirogues all by herself. Whose great-grandfather—Ndongo's great-great-grandfather—had taken a genie wife. Whose magical power was to expand when angry or in charge, balloon in a way you could not physically pinpoint, somehow taking up all the space without visibly changing, a kind of intangible human blowfish. A force more terrifying, sometimes, than the sea.

Maaleikum salaam, Madame Fatou. I am Anna. I am a writer. I am here to research a book about fishing.

That's great! *Bismillah, bismillah.* May you have luck in your work.

We shook hands.

How is the sea?

I don't know yet. I only arrived this month. I'm looking for a pirogue to take me fishing.

And Ndongo said:

Come with me tomorrow. We leave at six, rain or shine. We meet by the water, near the *mbaar.*

He grinned. He had his mother's smile.

By noon the sun burns hot. The batik sky condenses toward the horizon and weighs down the ocean edge with black storm clouds. Upon the water, pointing in all directions like matchsticks randomly spilled out of a box, sway hundreds of fishing pirogues.

The *Sakhari Souaré* spends the afternoon chasing fish. The dance of fingers, the flight of arms. Bubbles, bubbles! Fish are jumping! Big fish, a school!

Only Ndongo speaks.

They're close they're close.

Then, quieter still:

Cast net cast it cast cast—cast.

Spray and seaweed fly at the stern and the boys knock at the fish so hard the red covering board of the port gunwale dances. Both little Maguette and Vieux splash into the sea, but Ndongo says Ousmane can't go. You are a man, so work like a man. The boy pouts. Ndongo drops anchor and trawls it along the ocean floor: this will scare bottom fish into the net. The net comes up gleaming with bonga shad, each perfect. A full gillnet hauled aboard: a waterfall streaming upward, a silver breath sucked in.

▽ ▲ ▽

Watch the sea.

Arms by their sides, arms folded, hands in pockets, they watch. The tide is coming in. The *Sakhari Souaré* casts net again at two-thirty-two, three-thirty, four-oh-eight. She hauls snakelike halfbeak, Spanish mackerel with razorlike gills, a phallic mangrove fruit. Catfish, seaweed, more shad, nothing. The horizon glows golden, a thin unreal slash across the storms. Thunder; younger boys duck their heads in reflex. A pelican flaps with determination westward. Vieux tears off a piece of mackerel fish tail, sticks it in his ear, twirls, removes some earwax, then scampers over to port and relieves himself into the pirogue's bubbly wake.

The tide turns again. A thick gray column of rain stands over Joal. The sea is the same faded green as the net, and the crew are barely awake, sprawled or hunched all over the boat. Time to go back. At the bow Maguette the elder washes his face and arms and feet with seawater, sits down sideways on the forward thwart facing tentatively toward Mecca, and prays.

With a dramatic sigh Ousmane falls backward into the wet net, shuts his eyes. But Ndongo rouses him—what a lazy-ass kid!—calls him over to the stern, explains how to steer to harbor. Past the shipwreck at two-thirds of a throttle. Past two sea turtles and a large pelican pod—a hundred or more in flight, a few dozen in a baobab tree, pale pink in the queer light of a stormed-over afternoon. Past the Seven Baobabs, a salt flat just north of Palmarin where five centenarian baobabs grow in a circle, sheltering more pelicans; no one seems to recall when there were seven. A rainbow now arcs above the spot. Careful after the baobabs, the tide's going out, don't get stuck on the shoals.

Ndongo retrieves a cellphone from the mayonnaise bucket and calls a shrimper.

Hey, man, it's Ndongo. Hey, you going out tonight? Good, my mother wants thirty kilos of shrimp. Thanks, man. God bless.

The *Sakhari Souaré* chugs northward with five boxes of fish onboard: double the catch of the day before, double the pay for the crew.

Ndongo says to me:

In Senegal, when you go to sea with someone new and get a lot of fish, we say that person is good luck. You're good luck!

The horizon is a black line, drawn with kohl. The world may end there. The world is ending. Two pirogues crawl along that line. Under their prehistoric keels, our sustenance, our inchoate first memories, our last hopes. Aboard their mahogany hulls, fishermen. Tightrope artists. Desperados. Dreamers.

Two

High tide heaves over thick rollers of seaweed, reaches for the refuse that Joal's housewives dump daily at the wrack in an uneven putrid line. Onion peels, fish bones, lamb bones, plastic bags, rain-soaked baby diapers, yesterday's rice. Wrackline, tideline, the line of domesticity. Streams of effluent streak black into charcoal surf. Ringed plovers pick through the trash on the brim of the gray sea, invisible in the gray-brown light of predawn but for an emerging sense of movement, a kind of limbic rapidity that is ungraspable the way a dream the moment you wake up is ungraspable, just out of reach.

▽ ▲ ▽

Ndongo squats by the lip of the sea. With the heel of his right palm he clears of garbage a narrow window of wet sand. There, with a forefinger, he writes seven times, left to right, the Arabic letter *waw*, the initial letter of one of the ninety-nine names of God, Wahabou: the Bestower, the Grantor of Bounties without measure, the conferrer of wishes. Ndongo calls it the Prayer of Seven *Waws*. It is the fishermen's go-to spell. Thousands of pirogue captains scribble it in the sand and write it in the air daily before hauling anchor. They paint it inside the hulls of thousands of pirogues whose crews go to sea along the West African seaboard, go to sea wanting.

Wanting. A habit born during the Cambrian explosion, when the Earth's oceans, advancing over her young continents and withdrawing again enriched by mineral plunder, brought forth the first animals, creatures that could move independently and of their own volition and that needed to eat other organisms to survive. Some of these animals would become fish; much later, hominids. They wanted food. An urge half a billion years old. All of us have it. To satisfy it, some of us still return to the sea.

Ndongo traces the *waws* in the tideline to count them, then gathers the wet sand into his right hand. Blows on it, closes his fist over it. Holds the fist high as he wades out to the *Sakhari Souaré* through swash of fishrot and torn plastic bags and foil cookie wrappers, climbs aboard astern, and hops so very lightly from thwart to thwart to the net hold. He lets the sand fall into the billowing green nest. This will ensure that the pirogue's motor won't break, that she will return to port safely, and that even if she does not catch a lot of fish at least her crew will not go hungry.

Amadou Souaré, Ndongo's father, says that a better spell than the Prayer of Seven *Waw*s is this one:

You draw in the sand a pentagonal star. Look, I'm showing you. You say a prayer for each of the triangles—here, and here, and here, and here, and here—and then you say a prayer for the center—here—and then you take a little bit of sand from each part, and then you blow on it, and then you take it aboard the boat with you. It's the same prayer that the Prophet Muhammad said, and that the Wolof, and Serer, and Bambara, and white people say. It goes: "There is no God but God and I pray to God and I pray to the Prophet. If there are a lot of fish, we will share it. If there are no fish, I will still get my part. Let me not return with an empty boat." This way you get God's blessing for your trip. You have to have God's blessing for everything.

For example. Many years ago there was a prophet named Younis. He went to sea without God's blessing. But there were too many men in the boat and they drew a lottery, and Younis pulled out the ticket that said he had to go overboard. So he went overboard and a giant fish, a whale, swallowed him.

Because he traveled without God's blessing.

Correct. In the belly of the fish Younis realized his mistake and he said, *La illaha illa Allah*, and the fish came close to shore and opened its mouth and vomited him out.

That's why we must do everything with the blessing of God.

Amen.

Ndongo whispers a different prayer to evict Kuus Kondrong, a small-time genie, a hunchbacked dwarf who sleeps in berthed pirogues. Kuus Kondrong must leave the boat before she sets out. If he remains onboard he might make mischief. He might make the boat capsize for no reason. He might make you drop your cellphone in the water. But if you touch his hump you will immediately become a billionaire.

▽ ▲ ▽

Once I watched from a distance as a fishing crew set out from a thicket of mangroves and Sodom's apples at Joal's southernmost point, where mudcrabs burrow in the boggy sand that uncovers only at low tide. Five men and two women had gathered by a beached pirogue. Then four of the men climbed aboard and the fifth pushed them off and walked away with the women. By the time I reached the launch site everyone had gone. In the pockmarked sand, a pentagonal star pointed toward the water. Thrusting out of the pentagram's heart, almost as tall as me, black and curving slightly, was a zebu horn.

▽ ▲ ▽

They say Serer farmers settled Joal a thousand years ago. A West African people whose polytheistic pantheon dated back to the Neolithic, they may have been fleeing south from the

Almoravid Berber jihad that would impose fundamentalist Islam from Spain to Ghana. They were not mariners, though they occasionally waded into the silty tidal pools to clam among the mangroves.

Change arrived by sea, as it often does. In the fifteenth century Portuguese missionaries and slave traders disembarked near Joal. A trading post for gum and slaves opened and shut and opened again. A Portuguese Catholic mission gave way to a Portuguese synagogue, then to a French Catholic mission. Sufi Islam, its mysticism harmonious with Serer pre-Islamic practices, finally took root—first the conservative Qadri, founded in twelfth-century Baghdad by the Persian Cheikh Abdul Qadir Jilani; then Tijaan, whose adherents believe that honorable intentions and good deeds and regular recitations of liturgy lead to God; and later Mouride, which espouses the sanctity of hard work; and Layenne, practiced almost exclusively by Lebou fishermen; today most Senegalese are Sufi Muslims, though in Joal several hundred people still go to Mass, raise pigs, and name their children after Christian saints. It is said that in the middle of the nineteenth century, on his way to launch the Toucouleur jihad and establish a shortlived empire in present-day Mali, the Tijaan Sufi scholar el Hadj Oumar Tall prayed in a tiny mosque by the Mama Nguedj, the tidal marsh at the eastern edge of town. It is also said that he prayed by the marsh and the mosque was erected later, in commemoration. Its bleak adobe cube slumps by rotting water at the lip of Tann Ba, the sweeping acrid field where women dry and hotsmoke shad and sardinella on long rickety tables. Dry season winds blow from the east: most of the year the fish smoke that rises above the mosque blows seaward, choking the town. Folks here call the fumes the incense of Joal.

By the time Senegal gained sovereignty from France, Joal was a village of about five thousand millet farmers. There was one fishing pirogue. It belonged to Ngo Dioh, a fisherman, a son and grandson of fishermen. Ngo is dead now. His son Djiby Dioh, an unhealthy man in his sixties, lives on the main street in a three-story house of tiled floors and tall mirrored windows tinted blue to keep out the sun. You can see the ocean from the top floors, you can smell low tide from the balcony. Djiby was fourteen when he first went to sea, right after independence. The trips were short then; you would leave after sunup and by midday the pirogue was full of fish. No foreign ships then in these seas, and hardly any local competition. Owning a pirogue, he says, was like owning a chunk of gold.

Then a terrible drought struck the Sahel. Crops shriveled, skeletal people laid their dead in roadside mass graves. In Senegal's starved bush, farmers and cowherds loaded onto donkey carts and caravanned seaward. Some were Serer; some Fulani, whose forebears had domesticated cow in the Horn of Africa ten thousand years earlier; many were Wolof, whose language is Senegal's lingua franca. This had happened before: Disgorged by the ocean onto dry land, a cumbersome and plodding prevertebrate evolved in forests and savannah grasslands and grew hungry and returned

a hundred and sixty thousand years ago from the depths of eastern Africa to the shore of the Indian Ocean as Homo sapiens.

When the twentieth-century refugees reached the Petite Côte
they learned that all the farmland was already taken. They had
nowhere to turn but the sea. Like their distant ancestors, these
landless people became fishermen.

Around the same time, the world's appetite for fish began to
grow. Global fish consumption would almost double over the
next half century; some of the fish for Western tables would be
hauled by pirogues like the *Sakhari Souaré*. The worst of the
droughts ended in the seventies but fishing remained lucrative.
Outboard motors appeared in Senegal, Johnsons and Evinrudes,
eight horsepower at first, soon forty. Shops began to stock mass-
produced nets as long as two hundred yards. Unlike the water at
ports farther north, where the southwestward gyre of the Canary
Current pummels the shore with towering breakers, the ocean in
Joal is tranquil, subdued by the west-flowing North Equatorial
Countercurrent and a continental shelf almost eighty miles wide.
Wolof and Lebou fishermen from the north who had once mi-
grated up and down the coast were relocating to Joal for good,
joining erstwhile farmers at the wharves. Among these fishermen
was Amadou Souaré.

Amadou came to Joal from Dakar in 1978 with his young
bride, Fatou Diop Diagne, his first. They were in their mid-
twenties. By then Joal had a population of around twelve thousand people and two or three dozen fishing pirogues.

A couple of years before Amadou Souaré moved to town, ocean surface temperatures had begun to climb, and the first big mechanized trawlers had come to fish offshore. Most fished illegally, without license and with impunity, scooping up first a fifth of Senegal's catch, then a third, then half, worth hundreds of millions of dollars each year. Fishermen who had been here awhile noticed changes in the sea. Entire species of fish would vanish almost completely that decade and the next—among them the totem sawfish, whose stylized image graces West African francs. The year Amadou arrived, Djiby Dioh stopped fishing off Joal altogether and began to go to Guinea-Bissau. Djiby has since retired; now his grown sons pilot his fleet of half a dozen seventy-foot gillnetters from Joal, their port of registry, into Guinean waters, going on trips that last two or three weeks. There is still some fish down that way.

Ndongo was born a few months after Amadou and Fatou moved to town. His sister Siny came a year later. Then Amadou took a second wife, the mother of Maguette the elder and Saliou and several other children. Then a third wife. A fourth. Recently he divorced that fourth wife, the youngest. He said it was because she would bathe in the evening and come to bed with wet hair. But his friends say he divorced her because he had fallen in love with a woman in Kaolak, a large town two hours away, and wanted to marry her, and Islam allows a man to have only four wives.

After Siny was born, Fatou had no more children.

▽ ▲ ▽

Amadou Souaré is sixty-three years old, with thick, arthritic bones. He never smiles for long. Like Djiby Dioh, he no longer goes to sea. Old men rarely do. They sit at the *mbaar* all day like seagulls, their gray heads turned to the ocean, and wait for younger fishermen to return to port and offer them deference, perhaps some stories, always some fish. Sharing the catch with grounded fishermen, young or old, is the protocol all along the West African coast. Misfortune can happen to anyone—a pirogue will capsize, a motor will break, or an arm. A lazy crew won't show up on time. Or you will need a day off. Or the rest of your life. But because fishers share, you can always count on having fish to bring home for your wives to cook. Or you can sell it at a markup and pay your electric bill. By the waterline no one goes hungry. Spent as it is, the sea still provides leftovers, bycatch, handouts, quick jobs.

That is how it hooks you: it always delivers, at least a little bit, at least for now. Its tug is relentless, like its tide. Even to be in its presence, its briny air. To lift your eyes and behold the spirit levels of its many onrushing lines, its attenuated seascape of inception.

When Ndongo is not at sea, he, too, spends his days at the *mbaar*. There is a kind of a similarity between fish and fishermen, he says. Fish are unable to leave the water. And fishermen are unable to leave the shore.

Year after year more pirogues flag to this harbor. Year after year more fathers pull their sons out of primary school to turn them into deckies. Ndongo's children—Amadou Souaré's grandchildren—are growing up in a town of almost fifty thousand people, mostly fishermen or future fishermen. Year after year there are fewer fish. When I ask my friends why they keep fishing they repeat a tired mantra: My grandfather's grandfather was a fisherman, my father was a fisherman, I am a fisherman, this is all I know. But I think that something other than family tradition is also pulling them to sea: an ancient desire, a genetic memory, a congenital curse.

Or maybe it is because we habitually cling to coasts. Ever since Homo sapiens returned to the sea we have been hugging the Earth's saltwater ecotones, traversing her kelp highways. A species of the edge. When we strayed inland it was never for long. Think of our relationship to the coast as an ebb-and-flow dance, a millennial pantomimic waltz of tides.

▽ ▲ ▽

B efore Serer farmers settled in Joal, someone else had lived here. Who? Unclear: the ocean's oscillations have wiped out much of the human record along this shore. Whoever they were, these marine foragers left more than two hundred mounds of clam and oyster shells among the brackish channels that vein the mangrove mudflats between the Petite Côte and the mouth of the Gambia River. Some of the mounds are thousands of feet long.

Two such mounds rise out of the Mama Nguedj, the tidal marsh that empties into the ocean just south of Joal. Both are made primarily of the hinged ark shells of the *Senilia senilis* clam: a tiny seawater bivalve that coastal fisher-farmers from Mauritania to Angola have harvested forever and scientists hope to use to reconstruct past climate fluctuations and human movements in West Africa over the course of history. One midden is now a thirty-acre heart-shaped village of tabby concrete homes, mosques, churches, bars, a nunnery, some pigsties. This is the Isle of Fadiouth, home to the Sacred Baobab, which never drops its leaves even in the dry season, and to King of the Sea, who never sleeps off the island. The Sacred Baobab is a totem responsible for rain and harvest; King of the Sea is a matrilineal sorcerer who negotiates with the local protector genii for calm seas and fish. Two wooden bridges link Fadiouth to the mainland, like veins, like arteries. One leads northwest to Joal. The second, spanning northeastward, connects the island to the other shell mound. This midden has no name. It is an active burial site where the Muslims and Christians of Fadiouth inter their dead under six feet of shell.

How old are these middens? Also hard to say. Maybe eleven hundred years, just a hundred years older than Joal. Maybe twenty-four hundred years, as old as the Hippocratic oath, Plato's *Republic*, the kite. Scientists presume that the largest shell midden in the United States, Turtle Mound, in Florida, is three thousand years old. But dating seashells is tricky. The sea alters the content of the carbon isotope used in radiocarbon dating, makes marine organisms appear much older. Yet it safeguards entire marine

mountain ranges from erosion—indeed, from the complete dem-
olition they would have faced on dry land. And what about ob-
jects that were underwater, then exposed, then underwater again?
The sea corrodes some things instantly to naught, preserves others
for eternity, challenges conventional perception of time, challenges time itself.

The middens gleam in the sun: prehistoric trash heaps, warped
and washed-out memories, bleached by age and salt.

▽ ▵ ▽

Mbaar Kanené has other regulars. Malal Diallo, a gillnetter
captain whose Fulani parents and grandparents and ancestors uncountable for thousands of years herded cattle upon the
oceanic tracts of the Sahel, and who doesn't talk much. Daouda
Sarr, who spends more time prattling at the *mbaar* than at sea.
Daouda has beached his thirty-foot gillnetter, the *Stacko Mbacké*,
a few yards away from the gazebo. A breach in the hull has kept
her aground for weeks. Daouda is vague about the origin of the
breach. One day he will get around to fixing it, but for now he
relies on donations from other fishermen and on selling giant
prize sheep from the small flock he keeps in a manger behind his
house around the corner from the Souarés. He names his sheep
biblically, for the most part—Shem, Samuel—though one is
named Phil Collins.

The *Cheikh Sadbou*, at a twisted port tilt in the sand next to the

Stacko Mbacké, belongs to Ndongo's best friend Vieux Sene, the namesake of Ndongo's second-oldest son. Vieux has a gray goatee and always wears a bluegreen tartan flat cap. He is always on the phone with someone; he hardly ever removes his white earbuds. He has to replace both gunwales on his pirogue and recaulk it, work that has been taking him months because he never has enough money to pay for materials. He has two wives, a handful of children. He resells the fish donated by the men who do go to sea and hires himself out to fix their nets. He sits in Mbaar Kanené for hours at a time enmeshed in someone's gillnet, which he stretches between his left hand and the big toe of his right foot, his right hand always working a shuttle, a knife, a line, his eyes always drifting from the net to the sea.

The men at the *mbaar* watch waves lift and lower the anchored pirogues and talk fishermen talk:

Compared with thirty years ago, today the ocean isn't scanty— it is empty. The young folk today have no idea what real fishing is. When I was fishing back then, I could sit at this *mbaar* and watch schools of fish run in the sea. That's how close the fish would come to shore.

The sea was much farther out back then. Where those boats are over there, that was still the beach.

It's because of the Western boats. The government allows them to fish here, or maybe they come illegally. They come every night, even during the months when we are not allowed to fish at night. The fish run away from them.

Their big boats have sonars to find the biggest fish schools. They have GPS pagers to mark the spot in the sea. They have so much horsepower.

I heard they dynamite the fish to stun it and take it to their countries.

Yes. And then there are the purse seiners—there used to be twenty of them in Joal, now there are two hundred. They catch all the fish that run away from the big boats. And when they don't catch the big fish, they go after the small fish, the juveniles.

Yes. They deplete everything along the food chain.

Yes. There aren't any fish left.

Men click their tongues: hear, hear. Downcoast a gaggle of naked preteen boys and one girl in a short printed dress bob in the low breakers, cast mosquito nets for shrimp.

▽ ▲ ▽

A rtisanal fishing is Senegal's main resource and main earner of foreign exchange. In Joal it is the source of life entire. Street vendors sell bananas and rubberized slickers from the same stalls; fishnet roofs chicken coops and fences saplings against goats. Everyone eats *ceebu jën*—rice and fish—for lunch every day: *ceebu jën* with grilled fish, *ceebu jën* with stewed fish, gumbo, fish in *maafe* peanut sauce. When mothers drop off children at daycare in the morning they discuss their husbands' latest haul. The catch is down to a tenth of what it was a decade ago.

I pay a visit to Lamine Ndong, Joal's *chef du village*, a position that is elected and largely advisory. We sit in metal lawn chairs in a quiet unpaved square by his house. Cordia trees in vermillion bloom line the square. Its sand is swept clean. There is a monument to Léopold Sédar Senghor, Joal's most famous son, one of the founders of the Négritude movement and the first president of Senegal. Three women are selling dried fish and fresh eggplant and limes from a folding table. It is just before lunchtime and no one else is about.

Lamine Ngong is an old man. His ancestors, millet farmers all, have lived here forever. I ask him about the connection between Joal and the ocean, about the shortage of fish.

People who have roots in Joal, like me—we are not fishing families, he says. Most people you see at the harbor, they may be living in Joal now, but they are not from here.

He falls silent. Wind rustles the trees. Perhaps he has misunderstood the question. I try again.

Not many real Joaliens go to sea. Most fishermen are from elsewhere. I'm just telling you. So that you know that there are a lot of migrants in town now.

There is a gust and fire-red blossoms fall on our shoulders, in our laps.

Perhaps another reason why fishermen spend their days in *mbaars* looking out to sea is that the sea does not question their origins or their journeys, does not discriminate, bestows and conceals its wealth in equal measure.

▽ ▲ ▽

Anyway, says Amadou Souaré, Ndongo knows the sea as it is today better than I do. I knew the sea thirty years ago.

Never the owners of knowledge but the custodians, the temporary stewards. You learn the sea the way you learn the spells—from your father, your uncles, your older brothers, other fishermen who hire you on their pirogues, the sea itself. You pass it on to your children, your crewmen, your friends at the *mbaar*. The knowledge is divided into the manifest and the hidden, and belongs only to God, and is collected only in the Koran. You can access it if you know where to look, if you are humble, and if you ask God's blessing.

What kind of knowledge does it take to depend on a resource so seemingly bottomless yet so palpably expended, to exacerbate its decimation each day you honor family tradition? And what is the protection against the crushing void of the ever-encroaching tide? Or against mostly illegal foreign ships that come in so close that on a clear night you can see from the beach their searchlights: eerie winks of a modern, mechanized organism that employs half a million people worldwide, vacuums the ocean empty, drowns out the ancient shanties of men who stubbornly chase fish in wooden boats?

The fisherman Daouda Sarr says there is a gris-gris so powerful it makes your skin impregnable like armor. If you are using this gris-gris and someone tries to stab you with a knife, the knife does not even scratch you. You make this gris-gris with the root of a certain plant, which you cook a certain way, then eat it or wear it in a special leather pouch.

What amulet is there for fish on the verge of extirpation—or for its hunters, who steer along the rim of rapid planetary-scale reordering in which entire cultures get subsumed, languages lost, songs forgotten?

▽ ▵ ▽

The last rains of the season squall in, squall out. Night's thunderstorm is blowing slowly out to a wine-dark, Homeric sea. The *Sakhari Souaré* follows. The crew breakfast on po'boys with boiled eggs and french fries, with *yassa*. Maguette and Vieux share a small bag of cookies. Pink cumuli rise above Joal, blossom in reflection. The last glance at the town before it disappears abaft: men washing horses in that blushing surf. The pirogue heads west-southwest toward her usual fishing grounds. For a minute or two, the discarded newspaper that held the po'boys and the brightly colored cookie wrapper follow in her wake. The water darkens then pales, becomes a chalky blue. The sky is asphalt gray. Done with breakfast, the fishermen stand up. Watch the sea.

Do they have an ocean like this in America?

Yes. They have three.

Then I don't get it. Why do they send foreign ships to fish in our ocean if they have three of their own?

The foreign ships are spacewarps. You can sail right up to

them, their floodlights can blind you, their hightech trawls can take your fish. Yet they are also out of bounds, fortressed behind the same impassable line as the rest of the West, which once forced millions of Africans over that dark boundary and now forcibly holds millions of Africans from crossing it. Some fishers turn their pirogues into smuggling vessels to take migrants to Europe. They become traffickers of men, latter-day Noahs. But lately, security at sea has been too tight. Coastguard cutters confiscate boats and motors, throw smuggler-fishermen in jail.

Besides, Europe is broke. Many of the men who crew pirogues in Joal have tried to make a living there but returned because in Europe there is no work.

Some of these men have worked on fishing ships. Trawlers flagged to Spain, to Portugal, to China. The conditions are hard, they say: shifts that go thirty-six hours at a time, fo'c'sles so cramped men must take turns sleeping, barely enough provisions, no shore leave; some men had their passports confiscated, were essentially placed in bondage aboard. The money is great. I once fished with a man who had worked on Spanish boats for twenty-five years, mostly out of Barcelona. His Spanish was flawless. He said he had made some good friends over there. Other than that he did not talk about the experience much. What would you say? How would you talk about a quarter century of living on the moon?

Secondhand stories are easier. Ndongo has one:

I know this one fisherman, he worked on a big ship for many months —for more than a year. He earned a lot of money and the captain knew he couldn't afford to pay it. So this captain, he decided to ditch this guy. One night this guy was in his bunk and he overheard the captain and the first mate talk about throwing him overboard. So he took a piece of paper, wrote down everything he'd heard, wrapped the paper in plastic, and hid it in the band of his underwear.

Aboard the *Sakhari Souaré* the crew are no longer watching for fish. Everyone has turned to Ndongo, listening. Weighing their options perhaps. Assessing the risks versus the benefits of joining the powerful fleet that harvests all the fish they cannot catch.

Ndongo continues:

A few days later the crew jumped him and threw him overboard. He was afloat for hours! Finally another ship picked him up—he was so tired by then he couldn't even swim anymore. When he recovered he told the people on this ship what had happened and showed them the proof, the piece of paper he had sewn into his underwear. The ship caught up with that first boat and got everyone arrested—oh, I'm so sorry about this, hold on!

A seagull has splattered my shoulder. Ndongo reaches over to wash off the mess with seawater. So, so sorry. Don't worry about it, I say. It's good luck where I come from.

Eww! Good luck? Saying that's good luck is like saying it's good luck if they throw you overboard!

The other fishers laugh. A relief, a distraction from the Odyssean urge to seek their fortunes across the waters, from the fear of what kind of prize may lie beyond.

I'd like to meet the underwear man, I say.

Well. I don't really know him. It's my friends who know him.

Once Ndongo was at sea on a pirogue that ran out of drinking water. There was a foreign fishing trawler on the horizon and the captain steered toward her. On the deck of that ship was a white swabbie. Ndongo's crewmates gestured for water and the man laughed and trained his hosepipe at the pirogue. For years Ndongo had a burn scar where the scalding water hit his arm.

▽ ▲ ▽

Oily seas, steep seas. Some spray, some drizzle, sticky curls of fog. No shore in sight. Sardinella schools too fast for the *Sakhari Souaré*'s underpowered motor. She casts three times, like men, like men, catches barely anything. A smooth-hound shark the color of a dove's wing, with vertical pupils, vulnerable to extinction. A halfbeak. A school of cassava croakers flies right over the net's headrope. If you kill the engine you can hear them beat their abdominal muscles against the swim bladder: *ngok ngok ngok ngok*. Ousmane curls up in the net between each haul, eyes shut, silently lip-synchs a Wolof rap song. Maguette the elder says:

Last year one of my cousins was fishing near here and caught ninety-five boxes of barracuda.

We wouldn't even be able to fit ninety-five boxes in this pirogue.

Yeah, he had to call other boats to help him take it to harbor.

The *Sakhari Souaré*'s own net is empty again except for three

fanged cutlassfish, their pliant blue scaleless bodies long and predatory; the Senegalese do not eat them but white people mill them
into flour to bake bread. Ndongo says it's really delicious.

Have you tried it?

No, but I've heard about it. Have you?

I've never even heard of it. Let me ask you something, though.
What's it like to catch fish to feed someone halfway across the
world?

He thinks about it.

Makes me feel useful.

A few years ago one of Ndongo's cousins, a trafficker, invited
him to pilot a pirogue smuggling people to Spain from Casamance, in southern Senegal. A free ride to Europe, some cash on
top.

That boat, she was all outfitted and ready to go. A lot of my
friends were on that boat. Then my father called me and said, you
have to come back. So I came back. My only dream at the time
was to go to Spain. Oh-oh-oh I really wanted to go to Spain. That
was the only thing I could think about back then!

And now? You still want to go?

Wallahi, yes, yes! That's my dream, really. I know some men
who went to Spain, they come back with money, build shops here
or start a business, leave it with their brothers, and then go back
to Spain to make more money. If I can go there, get a work permit, and find a job, I would work really hard, then come back a
few years later. I'd send money to my father so he can build me a
boat of my own.

A boat of his own. Ndongo has been working on his father's boats since he was eleven years old. When he has his own pirogue he will take his net, first wife Alassane, second wife Sokhna, and the nine living children he has sired with them and reunite with third wife Khady, whom Amadou kicked out of the house two months ago, for willfulness, even though Ndongo was at sea that day and Khady was already visibly pregnant with their second child. Amadou Souaré is headstrong that way. Then, after everyone is settled and happy, maybe Ndongo will take a fourth wife.

A boat of his own, to take out to test and tempt the sea, so exhausted of fish and so full of stories, dreamy and unattainable, like a tide forever going out, sucking you away with it, rocking, rocking.

▽ ▲ ▽

By eleven o'clock the *Sakhari Souaré* has been out for four hours and has caught practically nothing. Ndongo sucks his teeth. What the hell? There were fish here just yesterday.

Hey, what day of the month is it?

October first.

No, what day of the Wolof month is it?

The eighteenth of Tabaski.

Ah. Perhaps that's why. Fish like spring tide, at full moon, that would be the middle of the month, after that they go hiding. We're just past it.

Then, for the first time since leaving the shore, Ndongo notices Maguette, his twelve-year-old.

Eh! What in God's name are you wearing?

The boy came aboard this morning in a huge orange life jacket. Who knows where he dug it up. He gives his father an impish grin. Ndongo says:

You've got to take that thing off, man. You look like a child!

▿ ▵ ▿

The *Sakhari Souaré* is almost to the port in late afternoon when a pursenetter twice her size sails up to starboard. Homemade canvas tents and huge styrofoam boxes aboard, painted blue, yellow, green, red. The *El Hadji Amar Dieye* is off to sea for a week with a crew of twelve. Would the *Sakhari Souaré* spare some fish for their dinner?

Ndongo nods to Ousmane. The boy scoops some halfbeaks and shad into a bucket, maybe a third of the day's catch. He leans over the water, passes the bucket. No words are exchanged. No money. One day it will be Ndongo's turn to ask.

▿ ▵ ▿

Do you know this fish?

A sweltering noon at the *mbaar*. Beached pirogues squat over shriveled ultramarine shadows. A bit to the south fishers are unloading cuttlefish traps tied to white and blue flags from a horsecart. On the sideboards of the cart its owner has written the Shahada in Arabic script the colors of the rainbow to declare in motion his belief in the oneness of God in the spectrum of God's own creation. I have seen this cart deliver outboards to pirogues at dawn; now the bay horse stands unmoving, stupefied by the heat. Ndongo has taken a day off and is sitting under the tin roof with some old men: his father's friends, his friends' fathers. He pulls up a picture on his cellphone screen, passes the phone around.

A friend sent me this photo. I wonder if you can catch one of those here. It's a real fish! But I've never seen a fish like this before.

A fading seascape. Orange beach in the foreground. At the tideline, a voluptuous horizontal figure: the head and torso of a fish from which grows a pair of woman's legs, pale and sensuously curved. A modest blur over the creature's woolly pubis. The old men bring the screen close to their opaque eyes, suck their toothless gums in wonder.

Says Pa Yagmar Kane:

Such fish don't live in these seas. These things only live very far from here, maybe in Asia or Europe, where the sea is deeper. I used to watch documentaries about Europe, but I've never seen such a fish.

Says Pa Ousmane Sall:

There are fish in other places that are different from the fish we have here. It depends on the weather, on the air temperature, on the temperature of the sea. I saw animals in the north that have so much fur, if they came here they would die of heatstroke.

The phone returns to Ndongo. He plays with the screen, makes the sexy womanfish grow larger, closer.

I know a fish called Mami Wata, he says. The bottom is fish, the top is woman. Mami Wata, they catch it here sometimes. I've seen it. It looks like a young woman on the top: she has silky hair—like yours, Anna—and breasts, but the bottom is fish and at the end of her tail there are scales. Mami Wata, I've never seen anyone eat it. But there's another big fish, called manatee—we eat that, but it looks like fish, not like a woman.

Mami Wata is the protector genie of Guinea, says Pa Ousmane Sall.

No, of Côte d'Ivoire! says Pa Bara Diop.

Yes, Côte d'Ivoire, you're right.

But she is also the genie of all the ocean, says Pa Yagmar Kane.

A mischievous and demanding protectress of the seas, the symbol of lust and fertility, often cradling between her bare breasts a large snake that has represented divinity and wisdom and the occult since Eden, she governs the ocean as Watermama in Suriname and Maman Dlo in Guadalupe, Lasirèn in the Caribbean, Yemanya in Cuba and Brazil, the mermaid or siren in Europe. In Australia, she is Yawkyawk, and the serpent that keeps her company is a water spirit that may be her father, her spouse, or Yawkyawk herself.

I ask Ndongo to draw Mami Wata in my sketchbook. He explains as he draws:

Mami Wata has webbed hands. She has another web between her elbow and armpit, right here, so she cannot extend her arm fully. Only like this. Her skin is light, like yours.

I pretend not to hear that the sea goddess of Ndongo's fantasies is a long-haired white woman, force it to slip my mind. If I want to keep the company of men at sea I must always evade the confines and expectations of gender and race. For the most part, Ndongo and my other crewmates and neighbors play along, cross boundaries of convention by taking me aboard, treat me as a kind of a liminal creature. They let me haul and pick and bail as if I were another man, though all politely look away while I relieve myself into the bailing can.

I watch Ndongo draw. His strokes are so tentative I think at first my pen has run out of ink. Decades since the last time he drew on paper. The breasts of his Mami Wata are sad deflated triangles, like mine.

As for the thing on my phone, Ndongo says, usually they come from other countries.

One day a few years ago some fishermen from Mbour, a fishing port between here and Dakar, caught Mami Wata in their net. She spoke to them in a human voice and asked them to release her. They refused. They brought her to Mbour, where people at the harbor looked at her and touched her. Finally they killed her. The next day the pirogue whose crew had caught her capsized, and everyone onboard died. I heard some people in Mbour ate the meat. Anyway, your sketchbook is too small. Look, the tail is

much longer. And the whole
fish Mami Wata is really the
size of a normal woman.

Ndongo hands the sketch-
book back to me. The mer-
maid takes up the entire
four-by-six-inch sheet. Broad
face, a pyramid of wavy hair almost to the shoulders, those
spent breasts. Her massive tail
splashes off the pad somewhere. What did she taste like,
I wonder, fish or flesh? Ndongo
says:

I don't know exactly how they killed her. I never saw her, only
a photo.

And Pa Bara Diop adds:

In this life, people shouldn't say, This thing doesn't exist. They
should say, I haven't seen it yet.

▽ ▲ ▽

All the ancestral genii and saints gather at the Point of
Sangomar, a sand spit at the reticulated mouth of the Saloum
River Delta south of Joal. Few people have ever seen them up
close or know their shape, though it is said that the most terrible

of all, Mariama Sangomar, has three heads, six arms, and one leg. Genii usually appear to fishermen as moving lights that have no sound and leave no wake. The lights blink or shine continuously, yellow or white.

Daouda Sarr tells this story: One night he went fishing around Sangomar. A friend also came, in a pirogue of his own. At some point, in the dark, the friend saw a blinking light, assumed it was Daouda beckoning him, and followed the light into the labyrinth of mangroves. He was lost till sunup.

Spirits live in the sea because water transforms. To impregnate Danaë, Zeus penetrated her in the form of golden rain; their infant son, Perseus, bobbed in the waves in a wooden chest before washing ashore, where a fisherman adopted him. The Holy Spirit of Christians descends upon the baptized through water. The historian Martin Klein writes that in August of 1848, when the colonial administration of French West Africa posted notices that indenture had been abolished, the freed slaves in Saint-Louis, the colonial capital, rushed to the sea "for what seemed to have been a spontaneous ritual cleansing."

Genii cross over into the world of humans for all the reasons we venture into the unknown: to entertain and challenge themselves, to assert their power. In the name of love. For example, Vieux Sene's grandfather on his father's side had a genie wife. She lived in the ocean, off the coast of Saint-Louis. Whenever Vieux's grandfather wanted to visit that wife he would get into his pirogue, alone, and sail westward until no one could see him from the shore. When he would return he would say things like, My other wife sends her greetings, or, My other wife just gave birth to a new baby.

Ndongo's great-grandfather on his mother's side also had a genie wife. But after his death the family neglected her, and in punishment she plagued its women with spells of aphasia and anorexia. Ndongo's grandmother, the mother of Fatou Diop Diagne, was so afflicted. At last, with the help of a healer, Fatou figured it out and began to take care of the genie by giving her offerings of sweet millet porridge called *lakh*, and by giving alms of sugar cubes to *talibé*, young students from Koranic schools whose praxis mandates begging. Since then, women in her bloodline seem to have been doing fine.

The genie placed another curse on the family, one Fatou cannot oblate away: If a newborn baby resembles a parent, one of them does not stay very long. Either the parent or the baby dies. That's why, Fatou says, we put a bracelet on the baby's wrist, for protection. One day I was walking with my two sisters, and someone saw us and said, "You must have the same father!" because we look so alike. Now one of my sisters is dead.

Romance between humans and genii is common and commonly tragic. A besotted genie will use magic to make the beloved inaccessible to other people. Daouda has experienced this himself. He was engaged to a girl who one day started acting very strange. In the middle of their rendezvous she would suddenly zone out, become nonresponsive, fall absolutely silent. When Daouda would confront her about it the next day she would say, I really don't know why that happened, I don't remember it. These were clear signs that a genie had taken her as a lover, Daouda says. Special healers will hold exorcism ceremonies to break the link between the lover genie and its human victim; the healers are usually women from the Lebou fishing people, like Fatou Diop Diagne, and live mostly in Dakar. But Daouda's betrothed did not want to be healed. Perhaps that was because of the genie, too. Daouda had to break off their engagement.

Sometimes a genie will keep the human lover in the genie world. Vieux's oldest brother went fishing ten years ago and his pirogue vanished at sea. A marabout told the family that the young man was alive but a sea genie kept him for herself. Since then, on religious holidays, the family has been setting aside some of the sacrificial lamb for the genie, putting it in the sea, asking her to treat the young man well. Vieux's father used to make the offering on the ancestral shores of Saint-Louis—a two-day roundtrip by shared taxi from Joal. Now Vieux's father is dead and Vieux's mother continues to honor the genie, though she makes the sacrifice here in Joal.

How did the marabout know that Vieux's brother did not simply die at sea? Many fishermen do. I have gone to their funerals, I have seen their graves. The distinction remains impenetrable to me.

The men talk, hush, talk again. The clink and rasp of knives sharpening on the cement gillnet sinkers. The dull thunk of a knife notching a line. The exhale of Vieux's nylon thread tightening around itself. He is repairing a comrade's gillnet: a shaggy floatline has snagged the top. He removes it, notches a new half-inch headrope, and is weaving the blue nylon mesh onto it with a shuttle threaded with a dark blue fishline. He stretches the net between his left hand and his right big toe and his hands move so fast I cannot follow the pattern. An arachnid. A sorcerer.

Daouda looks at me.

Do you believe it, Anna? Do you believe that genii exist?

Why do you ask?

Because. In Senegal, if it has a name, then it exists.

Poïesis, creation, the making be. An unceasing initiatory song that enacts its magic again and again in countless individual instances of becoming: When a mother names everything to her infant. When new lovers point out to each other a moonrise, a sunset, a freckle, as if no one had ever seen these before. Look! Look! The command of complex language gave our forebears the cohesion to strike out of Africa, and they named to one another new coasts and landscapes as they narrated their way, stanza by millennial stanza, to Tierra del Fuego. Each story is foundational, each makes the universe afresh. Each is a trespasser: from nonbeing into being.

In stories, as at sea, boundaries are malleable, begetters and destroyers both. The genii who marry humans cross a permeable membrane between the sacred and the everyday. Like storytellers. I think: We hold the power of making magic real by how we engage it, by which stories we choose to tell. Or maybe the stories choose us.

▽ ▲ ▽

also often think that Daouda is testing me, pushing my boundaries. That maybe he himself is a trickster genie from the sea.

▽ ▲ ▽

On the third night of October, the twenty-first night of Tabaski, a savage squall rips through Joal. Broken tree limbs scythe power lines. Torn roofs hurtle like discuses. A child electrocutes on a live wire. Electricity and cellphone networks will remain down for two days. Early the next morning the alley where I rent a room from a retired fisherman is a murky ankle-deep puddle, but in seaside mosques disciples of Tijaan Sufi brotherhood, Senegal's most widespread, are already chanting their morning *wird*, the melancholy choral blessing and plea for forgiveness they recite twice daily. The roof in my quarters springs leaks and all night warm raindrops nag on the pillow and the floor by my head; the room is a tiny afterthought tucked between a pit toilet, a washroom, and a cinderblock manger, and by morning every surface inside is wet.

In the dark I leave the compound, wade through the puddle, and walk past the mosques two miles up the rainpacked shore to the *Sakhari Souaré*. It is six-thirty, low tide. Wet laundry sags from lines strung between beached pursenetters.

The east reddens. Branches and entire trees and tattered sheets of roof metal score the beach; dawn smells like rotting fish and eucalyptus. Mbaar Kanené is aslump: two of the bearing posts are broken. Aboard the *Sakhari Souaré* the twisted net is heaped all over the boat and full of seaweed, and in the holds two dead fish float belly-up in a mix of rainwater and bilge.

Maguette?

It wasn't me!

Boys bail center hold, make the boat shipshape again. The bilge pours black into the greening sea. Ndongo maneuvers through the marina. The *Maimouna Lo*, which belongs to his third wife's landlord, is shorthanded today, only four men, so Ndongo drops off Ousmane to be the *oupa*. The boy jumps from his father's gunwale onto the other pirogue, bellyflops into the net hold, stretches out on the net. Ndongo watches him, clicks his tongue. That boy.

Like a man, remember? he calls. And speeds off.

Mangroves float above the horizon. Green net, green waves. Ndongo sucks his teeth. The storm has changed the color of the sea, he says. It probably has dispersed the fish, too. They get scared into the sea when it gets windy like this. This is never easy: we bought fuel, my crew are investing effort, and the *Sakhari Souaré* probably won't catch much today. But she must try.

Because of greed. Because of curiosity or penitence. Because of inertia, even, maybe. The wooden pirogue slips away from Africa.

Mamadou Faye, new onboard, winks at his captain from the bow. Mamadou is twenty-eight, an affable tall ironsmith who usually works for his mason father. But because there have not been many fish in the sea, fishermen have not been building new homes, which means there has been no construction work ashore lately, and so here he is, crewing Ndongo's pirogue, even though last month his own younger brother, Abdoul Ahad, went fishing for the first time and never returned. The family waited a few days, then held a memorial service. No genii meddling there. A death at sea, simple and stark and irreparable.

Ndongo? says Mamadou. Wouldn't it be nice if we got ten boxes of large mullet today?

I personally am hoping for some sardinella, says Ndongo.

Mamadou laments in singsong:

So hard for young people to find work nowadays that you have to know how to do everything. You have to be a jack-of-all-trades, have at least two professions, better three or four—

At night sardinella schools glow in the sea, you can see them, Ndongo interrupts. He stares and stares at the waves, his gaze distant, full of something that looks like lust.

—so if one doesn't work out you can fall back on something. All I want is fancy digs, a fat SUV, and an import-export permit.

The wishes of the era, no more lasting than a trace in the waves. No more shallow than hunger, hunt, survival.

At ten in the morning Ndongo commands:

Cast net.

The gillnet sinks into a black black sea. An hour later the crew begin to haul. Mamadou starts a shanty:

Don't talk but work—don't talk but work—and catch it—quickly—and catch it—quickly—like men, like men—quickly—like men!—And all together now—and don't hold back—and all together now—and don't hold back—

Hand over hand, the crew pull yards of empty green mesh out of the sea—and then.

Suddenly.

Two, three, four fish in every square foot of net, jerking and twisting, rubbery, hard, all tight muscle like coiled springs. Sardinella! Sardinella! So many fish that Ndongo whoops and dances from the stern to midships and joins the picking. Round sardinella, *Sardinella aurita*, silver with a faint golden mid-lateral line from the gill opening to the tail like a drizzle of oil, like the trace of a sunray. Mamadou grins, switches the rhythm:

Sardinella, sardinella—it is here—sardinella!—If you don't go out for fishing—you can't eat no—sardinella!—Let's all eat our—sardinella!—come on, let's eat—sardinella!—*Tout le monde* eats—sardinella!

The sun slants and the ocean is black and silver like fish scales and the crew pick a full net and laugh and sing:

My father I'm crying—why are you crying—excuse me, why you crying—oh, child, why are you crying?—Work like a motherfucker—I work like a motherfucker—work like a motherfucker—oh, child, why you crying?

Rounds made up on the spot. Worksongs as old as fishing.

The holds are full and blood sloshes in the bilge. You can tell sardinella by the bail: no other fish bleed this much. Ndongo looks up, squints sternly, points to the east. On the horizon another boat is hauling net. In his quiet captain voice he says:

They got more fish than us. Because they didn't miss a school like we did.

For man at sea is unquenchable. The vicious adrenaline rush that accompanies the hunt for fish is like nothing I ever have encountered anywhere else. Not even in war zones, where for many years I watched reckless boys chase death, have I seen men so monomaniacal. Fishermen: the most rapacious people I know. In their avarice, merciless. Mamadou lets the jibe pass, winks at his crewmates, picks net, sings on:

If you want to be strong—eat couscous!—If you want to be strong—eat couscous!

After midday Ndongo pilots the *Sakhari Souaré* south toward the shipwreck of Palmarin.

▽ ▲ ▽

Daouda Sarr, who grew up in Palmarin, was a teenager when white foremen brought black crews and tractors and bulldozers to build an asphalt road between his village and Joal. Every night the crews would hammer wooden stakes into the clay to mark the future route, and every morning they would return to find the stakes torn out and tossed roadside.

The foremen blamed the locals. Palmarin elders said genii were pulling up the stakes because the white people were building the road on sacred land. One time, the foremen decided to spend the night on the site, hoping to catch the saboteurs. After darkness fell, a disembodied voice appeared to the contractors as if in a dream and ordered them to build the road elsewhere. Only then did the contractors reroute the road to a land not claimed by spirits, where it lies today in potholed disrepair, barely passable during the four rainiest months of the year.

Sakou Sarr, a Palmarin village elder, tells the story of the road differently:

Our village has been here since the twelfth century, though older middens exist. After the local population adopted Christianity and Islam, polytheistic beliefs remained. There are local totems. Write their names: Balfany, Fatou Ngous, Nanai, Tioupan. He dictates the names slowly, waits for me to take them down. The totems require offerings of milk and beer, some prayers to secure good crops and a safe rainy season. When villagers have troubles they appeal directly to the totems.

In 1978 when white people were trying to build a road they faced two complications. One, this is an area of extreme salinity. And two, when they began the construction they ignored the totems and failed to offer a sacrifice to the spirits. That's why they had problems. For example, some of their equipment that worked just fine yesterday wouldn't work today. Or their cars would run today but tomorrow would stall for no explicable reason. But after they made an offering all such nuisance stopped and they were allowed to build the road.

As for rerouting the road to appease the genii, Sarr has never heard such a story. Some people exaggerate, he says.

Sakou Sarr's big house is decorated with images of Pope John Paul II, of Pope Francis shaking hands with Senegal's president, Macky Sall. There are plastic Santa dolls and fake plants. In the hallway, his teenage children—a beautiful girl in a long black skirt and a black bra, who studies geography in Dakar; and her younger brother, a high school student, in shorts—are watching a concert of traditional music on TV. I can smell someone cooking *ceebu jën* for lunch in an indoor kitchen behind a closed door.

A block from the house the jinxed tarmac road runs past sky-blue mirror of estuaries that sparkle with an astonishment of egrets, pelicans, yellow weavers. Tiny red passerines hover like suspended droplets of blood. The other village streets are clean deep sand. The seaside is all villas that belong to seasonal Europeans, cheap seaside lodges, former homes half eaten by the encroaching sea, palm groves, the Seven Baobabs at the northern tip. The beach is paradisiacal. From here, the rusted hull of the shipwreck is a random theater backdrop, a misplaced decoration, like Sakou Sarr's Christmas ornaments in October. I ask him about it.

It shipwrecked near here in 1978. Same year as the road.

Same kind of problem?

Perhaps.

⛢ ⛢ ⛢

The shipwreck of Palmarin is not marked on the geodetic datum chart of the Atlantic coast between Saint-Louis and the Saloum River, which shows one hundred and twenty-nine other wrecks. Nor is the wreckage of the slave ships that sank during the four centuries of transatlantic slave trade carrying Africans to the Americas. Tens of thousands of people stolen from these shores carpet the ocean floor with their bones.

⛢ ⛢ ⛢

Next to the Seven Baobabs, two or three hundred pelicans rise from the turquoise surf in elaborate and lordly synchronicity at the *Sakhari Souaré*'s approach. They head straight for the pirogue, the whole tremendous mass of them, low and menacing like bombers on a sortie—then suddenly swivel across her bow and back inland and settle in the tree crowns. A lone bird remains bobbing in the surf.

It can't fly!

Fly! Fly, bird, fly!

The giddy crew stand up in the boat. Naked from the waist up or in torn secondhand tee shirts; little Maguette's says LET'S KISS. Their arms and faces shine with sweat and fish scales. Fish blood streaks their rubberized overalls, elbows, necks. A ghastly circus troupe temporarily distracted from some grotesque ungodly act. They turn to the bird as one and begin to flap their arms in a freakish and profane simulation of flight, and Ndongo grins and comes about so roughly that the crew nearly topple and steers toward the pelican.

The bird spreads its wings, tipping backward to lift a white abdomen out of the water. A display; we watch. Its long lower mandible is yellow, its upper mandible gray, its breast a brownish gray; its primaries are black, and its secondaries and throat and tail and mantle and back are white. Then, in slow motion at once exquisite and scornful, it pushes itself off the water with large pink webbed feet two, three, four times and flies away.

Wow, says Mamadou.

Only young Vieux remains seated on the stern thwart. He has stuffed a piece of yellow styrofoam float into the mouth of a palm-size sardine, bound it in fishing line. Now he is threading the line with fishhooks. A torture victim, bound and gagged; a piscine Saint Sebastian.

What's this for? I ask. The boy looks up from his handiwork. He is beautiful, his eyes wide, inspired, deep as the sea. He says:

I want to catch a pelican.

▽ ▲ ▽

Less than a mile from Joal's harbor Ndongo spots a school running southwestward. He careens hard aport, then remembers he is inside a marine protected area designed to replenish fish stocks. All fishing is prohibited within five miles of the shore. Most crews fish here anyway. The enforcement of the sanctuary is lax, corrupt, and arbitrary. Fishermen take their chances: fishing is like gambling. Ndongo sets course again for the harbor, then suddenly drops the throttle, reaches into the sea to starboard with both hands, and pulls out a grouper the size of my thigh.

▽ ▲ ▽

With her bilges full of sardines and bloody water, the *Sakhari Souaré* slices into the harbor stubble of large and small pirogues unloading their catch. Ndongo runs her hard aground bowfirst between the dainty spindle of a clam boat and an enormous purse seiner. Immediately little Maguette jumps off the bow and splashes ashore to wedge the anchor in the sand.

Already fishwives in bright multilayered headwraps and embroidered velvet bonnets are rushing down in a determined stream from the bulky concrete façade of the harbor building a hundred yards or so inland. Their feet are bare upon warm sand slimy with fishrot and gasoil and effluent, and they wear long sleeves under torn, stained décolleté frocks that are soaked through from the armpits down. Skipping to the water with empty basins and buckets on their heads and under their arms, and some with babies and toddlers strapped to their backs, and some with lips busy around miswak toothpick twigs cut from a mustard tree, and some with mouths bright orange and grainy with kola nut. They negotiate the row of a dozen wheeled kiosks where hefty middle-men in large silver rings and heavy gris-gris bracelets drink instant coffee with milk or café Touba spiced with grains of selim and cloves. And then another row of kiosks that sell gloves, cell-phone recharge cards, memory cards with bootleg music downloads, waterproof cellphone pouches. They push through a row of twenty or thirty carts waiting to take fish to the ice-packing factories out back, where eighteen-wheelers dripping diesel and bloody slush load for Dakar, and skip around the freaked-out horses that stomp and back up in their harnesses, hides plastered with seaweed and fish scales. Around other fishwives squatting next to heaps of mullet, catfish, octopus, shrimp, grouper, sardines, and the obscene protrusions of cymbium snails, and the elegant tracery of purple-tinged murex. They wedge past itinerants selling baby clothes and imported secondhand skirts and blouses, and boys carrying the portable storefronts of wooden

glass-topped cases with costume jewelry, and other boys carrying garlands of dry dates and peanuts and cashews in small plastic bags. They exchange some brief jokes with young girls in tight denim and tanktops who sell coconut candy and beignets. Lastly, they excuse themselves past the modestly dressed restaurant owners, all women, who keep patient rank right by the water in anticipation of a wholesale deal for their evening kitchens. They wade toward Ndongo's pirogue.

Immediately other fishwives peel off from other boats where they have been bargaining unsuccessfully and join the cluster, up to their chests or armpits in the sickly yellowgreen muck that is more harbor refuse than seawater, the women with children careful not to wade in too far, ducking occasionally face-first to freshen up. They begin a singsong that is part mockery, part sweet talk. They call Ndongo their cousin, their brother, their lover, their father, their friend—their best friend. Male porters join in, in rubberized overalls and slickers and rubber boots that go up to their thighs and rubber cushions they affix to their heads with chinstraps made of boatline or torn from discarded women's dresses. Cart drivers, all men, whip their horses into this waterlogged crowd, spraying water. All of them bargain hard and loud against one another and against Ndongo for the catch, salty-tongued and cajoling, firing insults and praise and coquetry at the captain and crew and one another in Wolof and Serer and French.

Ndongo considers all of them regally and calmly, smiling at the women occasionally but in silence, until the porters who work for his regular middleman swim up. He orders his crew to help them load the sardines, keeps careful watch that no box be piled above the brim. Fishermen are paid per box.

The porters take turns balancing the boxes of fish on their

head cushions and swimming them to shore. Little Vieux bails. A gillnetter anchors next to the *Sakhari Souaré* and the gaggle of fishwives and porters migrates there. Little Maguette, wearing only wet drawers, returns aboard with plastic baggies full of hot café Touba for the crew and some beignets wrapped in newspaper for his dad. Ndongo sells the bycatch—the grouper he noodled out of the sea, a couple of halfbeaks, some mullet—to two fishwives. They will wade back ashore and resell this fish: to the restaurant owners at a fifty-percent markup; to the middlemen, twofold; threefold markup to the more squeamish buyers on the other side of the harbor building, beyond the fetid pools of fish guts and horse piss and truck fuel and melting ice.

Ndongo calculates the day's earnings: two shares for the motor, two shares for the boat, one share for the food for the house, where most of the crew sup, the rest divided equally between the fishermen aboard. He hands a banknote to Ibrahima, his nephew, and sends him with an empty plastic jerrycan to fill for tomorrow's trip. He is done here.

Maguette. Haul away on that line.

The sun rolls behind the sea and for a spell the clouded west blooms in a peony sunset. The salty horizon line powders and fades. Hugging the coast, the *Sakhari Souaré* sails southward to her berth near Mbaar Kanené at half throttle. Far away, southward also, an unending scarf of migratory birds flows down the East Atlantic Flyway. I imagine them girdling the Earth, pole to pole. It is autumn in Europe.

⩔ ⩘ ⩔

When Ndongo returns to shore he learns that last night's storm felled a filao tree onto the Souarés' second gillnetter, the fifty-two-foot *Ndaye Adja Kane*, named after Amadou Souaré's mother. She had been beached a hundred yards north of Mbaar Kanené, waiting for a paint job and some caulking. Now her hull is smashed flat by a tree white people brought to colonial Senegal to keep it from sliding into the sea.

In the dusk girls on skinny legs are rushing about the broken pirogue like plovers, picking up painted redwood splinters for firewood.

Three

Pirogue fragments are splayed out in an impromptu dry dock, a patch of beach sand littered with strips of net, swatches of tar-blackened cloth, splinters of broken boats, sheep droppings. The thick log of her keel points out to sea. Fanning slightly outward from either side of the keel lie maroon boards of fresh wood and scuffed painted boards of the pirogue that was, that will be again.

On the sand next to this once and future boat, a disassembled gull skeleton. A tipped translucent keel bone, broad and smooth and concave; around it the radii, the ulnae, the heavy curved beak. Somehow this fragile assortment of ossifications and tunneling pores was made to lift up and stand motionless in wind currents hundreds of feet in the air and from such balanced height to see past the dazzle of the waves, to identify fish underwater, calculate vectors—then plummet vertiginously, impossibly, and impossibly rise back up.

Somehow, too, this heap of mismatched wood will be made to sail and hunt fish. The new pirogue will fit two gillnets, even three, of different caliber. She will fit a lot of fish in her holds. What master shipwright Ousmane Ndoye is building: a possibility, a promise, a hope.

▽ ▲ ▽

Master Ndoye is a large man, with large hands. He has three teeth. He is sixty-three years old. He learned boatbuilding from his father and uncles as a child, and he has been a shipwright for more than half a century. He speaks Wolof and English and French, but he speaks little: Anna, hammer. Anna, nails. It's a hot day, bad for circulation.

He lives in Mbour, half an hour north of Joal by shared taxi, but he is charging less for his work than Joal carpenters because he and Amadou Souaré go way back, to the time before Ndongo was born.

We get the same age, Master Ndoye says, in English, rubs his thick grooved forefingers together to indicate closeness. I mishear: We get marriage.

Master Ndoye built Amadou's first pirogue. He will rebuild the *Ndaye Adja Kane.*

His tools are two hammers, a pair of pliers, a mallet, an ax, a small handsaw, a ratchet strap. His drill is a loaner from a hardware store a hundred yards inland, on Joal's single asphalt street—the longest one, the only one with a name, Boulevard Jean Baptiste

Collin, after the town's first post-independence mayor, a white Frenchman; the street parallels the shoreline all the way to the bridge to Fadiouth. The selfsame shop rents Master Ndoye a socket into which to plug the drill, and the three extension cords that connect it to power. From time to time horses and small livestock uncouple the extension cords.

Sometimes one of his carpenter sons comes by to help, but assistance mostly comes from whoever happens to be around: Ndongo; fishermen who are not at sea that day; children who come to gawk after school; me. He is patient with ineptitude: he has taught more than fifty shipwrights all over West Africa's coast north of the equator. His apprentices have taught apprentices of their own. Master Ndoye is the grandfather of an untold fleet of boats that catch your seafood from Nouakchott to Conakry. You can tell their multitudes by his stamp: a slender semioval cutout at the bottom of the bowsprit.

A West African fishing pirogue is carvel-built, constructed without a frame. Clammers and cuttlefish jiggers, narrow and light, are usually built with abachi, cheap white wood that does not last very long in seawater; luthiers use it to give electric guitars a bright, flinty sound, and a tincture made from its bark is said to reduce edema in pregnant women. Larger pirogues are built with Senegal mahogany, *Khaya senegalensis*, a redwood that grows in Casamance. The Dufana pirogue, an eight-thousand-year-old dugout boat discovered in Nigeria, was built with such redwood.

Senegal mahogany's bitter bark is said to cure leprosy and insanity and smallpox, its glabrous leaves malaria, its small white pedicellate flowers syphilis, its flat-winged seeds fever. It is being logged mercilessly for illegal export to China, where factories build fancy furniture with it. It is not reforested. They say it may vanish from Senegal completely before the end of the decade: overexploited wood to hunt overexploited fish. And then what? Will the pirogues be rethought? Will fishing?

The carpenter says, in English:

I want Ndongo to have a very nice boat. A very nice boat. Ndongo is a very fine man.

He rabbets the keel with an ax. Beneath the weathered surface the wood is the color of tuna flesh. He paces its length, traces the bearding line with a forefinger, chews his bare gums, marks something with a scrap of pink tailor's chalk.

Anna, drill.

He drills holes in the bearding lines; here he will attach the garboards, which form the bottom level of a boat's hull. Tars the ends of metal dowels, each two feet long, and hammers them into the holes obliquely upward. Precision-chisels a plank of new redwood to make a mortis, drills holes in that. This will be the port garboard. The angle of the holes determines the gradient at which the planking will project upward from the keel. He calculates it by feel.

Anna, hold.

He beads the garboard at a bevel onto the keel. Pounds it flush to the keel with a mallet. My shoulders lurch with each strike.

Old fishermen circle the boat. Toothless, in long pale boubous and sunglasses. They place their palms on the keel, caress it, give it a slap.

A thick keel is good, says Pa Bara Diop.

This is good, a good thickness, but if it were thicker it would have made a better pirogue, says Pa Yagmar Kane.

Yes. It would have been able to carry more fish, says Pa Ousmane Sall.

Master Ndoye says nothing, his lips tight around a half dozen nails. The job should take two weeks, maybe three. Just in time for the night-fishing season, which opens on the first of December. Fishermen swear that once the night-fishing season begins, life will be good. There will be much more fish in the sea, more money in fishermen's pockets to buy even more powerful motors and bigger nets with which to catch more and more and more. How can they be so sure? Because fish are always about to arrive, and wealth, like the sea, is always imminent.

But Amadou Souaré wants to reuse as much as possible the broken old wood from the shattered pirogue. He borrows from banks and begs middlemen for advances that always are too small. He scrimps. He scavenges for wood along the tideline. He buys cheap nails, which bend and break. He waits for a bigger catch, a better deal on wood. The construction will take two months.

▽ ▲ ▽

Ndongo quit school and became a fisherman in sixth grade, when he was eleven. Listening to the teachers' incomprehensible French was boring, listening to the jingle of coins in his pocket was not. By the time he was fifteen, Ousmane's age, he was fed up with the sea, the fishing, with his father's constant dictatorial nagging aboard. He asked Amadou's permission to return to school.

My dad said, No way. You are my firstborn son; if I don't have you, I don't have anyone to fall back on. You are a fisherman now. So I am a fisherman now.

That year Ndongo captained his father's pirogue for the first time. He had to remember which fish prefer the sunless bottom bed at low tide and which disappear entirely for the two weeks bracketing a full moon to burrow into the gooey silt at the roots of the mangroves. He had to remember that a full moon always brings strong winds and confused seas; that wind also picks up just before the new moon, during the last three days of each Wolof month; that if cuttlefish fishermen find pomfret in their traps it means a storm is coming. That in hot weather fish rise to the surface and in cold weather fish cluster around something underwater: seagrass, shipwrecks. He had to learn the Prayer of Seven *Waw*s and remember and repeat the words his father used to encourage the crew to cast and haul. Like men. Like men. Married by his father to his forefathers' sea that ebbs and flows of its own heartrending accord. Like many unions on these shores an arranged marriage, indentured and indisputable. Each year following he would thread some new knowledge onto the old, the way he would thread new protective amulets onto his gris-gris belt: which caliber gillnet to buy in October for the petite yellowtail and round sardinella and which in February, when the larger, oilier Madeiran sardinella start running; how big fishing ships change the patterns of fish migration; how to use a GPS—though he has not used his in months; it is broken.

Eh! Sometimes I want to leave the sea. It's such hard work for so little pay. In the winter, when we start going to fish at night, we will leave before noon, cast net around five, and return by six in the morning. There will be only time to buy provisions and fuel for the next tour and head back out. Six months of night fishing, six months of that! Sometimes our eyes feel funny. But what would I do if I'm not a fisherman? All I know is this.

A family hex, a genetic predilection.

Ndongo is eating a po'boy with boiled potatoes and fried onions at a breakfast cabana halfway between Mbaar Kanené and Master Ndoye's improvised shipyard. The vendor is the beautiful Mariama Boye. Twenty-five years ago Ndongo and Mariama's husband, Gora Sall, the son of Pa Ousmane Sall, were *oupas* together; now each of them captains pirogues. From before sunrise until eleven or until the food runs out Mariama sells breakfast to fishermen here at Mbaar Atelier Taïf, named after Taïf the outboard motor mechanic who takes over the gazebo in the afternoon. Sailors swagger in to buy a sandwich or a cup of milky café Touba, to flirt with Mariama, make small talk, watch the sea.

Hot today.

Yes. But I feel like it's cooling down.

Well, it's the end of October.

Yes.

Well.

In November it will be cooler.

Yes.

Yes. When it gets cold I get asthma. I hear that the inhaler is addictive, so I try to stick with traditional medicine, some tinctures.

I hear fish oil is good for asthma.

Yes. Fish oil is good for everything, especially memory.

Yes.

The Souaré children come by. Moustapha, twelve years old, Ndongo's nephew, likes history and is a diligent student. But his hair is natty and yesterday his teacher told him that he must cut it before he returns to school. When he came home, his father flew into a rage and said this was bullshit, no one is cutting Moustapha's hair, ever, and if that means the kid is not going back to school, then so be it. Moustapha's father is trouble. He drinks cheap fortified wine and smokes weed. He harasses Ndongo's wives, especially Alassane, his first; now whenever Ndongo spends a night with one of his other wives, Alassane sleeps with a wooden club by her bed. Moustapha's father spouts obscenities in the house. Once he was so foulmouthed the family had him arrested; the gendarmerie called Amadou Souaré to post bail. Moustapha wants to be a gendarme. Little Maguette wants to be a soldier. He has been back in school for a week now, in fourth grade. His older halfbrother Vieux will not go back to class: he wants to be a fisherman.

Ousmane wants anything but the sea. He got good grades until, three years ago, the pirogue was shorthanded for a month and he had to go fishing with Ndongo. He had money for the first time in his life, and that was that. But now he is making inquiries. Could he return to public school after dropping out in sixth grade? How much would a private school cost? When do classes begin? Around his father he is listless and monosyllabic. He listens to Senegalese rap and picks his lip into a discolored bulging misery of new infected cracks. His grandmother Fatou Diop Diagne takes him to a marabout who prescribes an aloe vera salve and some prayers. Nothing helps.

It's a good thing if among the brothers there is one who is not a fisherman, Fatou says during one of her evening walks, a daily thirty-minute promenade along the shore her doctor has recommended for hypertension. A clean shot to the sea from the house where she lives with Amadou, his second wife, their many children and grandchildren and inlaws, and hired crew, which traditionally bunk and sup with their captain. When I ask her how many people live in the house she takes a minute to add numbers on the calculator of her cellphone, then announces the tally: thirty-eight.

Fatou can see the ocean and some pirogues from the threshold of her compound. Four blocks to the sea down an alley of red soil studded with shells and caverned with deep green puddles many months old. There Fatou turns northward, walks briskly to the harbor along the tideline, surveys with barely a turn of her head the pandemonium of horsecarts, of rushing porters dripping wet with boxes of fish on their heads, of fishwives squatting on tarps beside piles of fish, of women selling charred corn on the cob and peanuts, and declares that there isn't enough fish.

You see? Fishing is too unreliable. You need to have an alternative. I would pick Ousmane to be that brother who does something else because he is the most intelligent of them all.

Ndongo shrugs at the efforts to cure Ousmane's lip. He says the boy's real affliction is indolence. He's not a hard worker, he says. Maguette and Vieux—they are hard workers. If they want to study I will be happy to pay for their education. But Ousmane, he is just lazy. I can't even send him to other boats in good conscience because I need to teach him first to work harder.

I think of my son, a boy on the cusp of adulthood struggling to adjust to university life on the other side of the Atlantic. Of my single-parent joys and heartaches during the years we did live together, of my regrets and pride now that we are apart. When is what we want for our children truly for their own good and for it alone—and when it is also for us, to reassure us that we have raised them properly, that we were good enough parents, to satisfy our vanity? Is there such a thing as selfless parental love? Do we take ownership of their successes and failures out of empathy and unalloyed affection, or do we see them as reflections of our own? Is it ever possible to know? Ndongo says:

Maguette here—he gets really good grades. He is always among the top five of his class. In composition, for example: that boy's a writer, like you! But Ousmane? He was so-so. All I ask of

Ousmane is that he be serious—whether at work or at school. I believe in making an effort. Even if he isn't good I want to see effort. I think he'll go back to school, he'll like it, then in two or three months he will lose interest. So we will discuss tonight.

And Master Ndoye, who is waiting for Mariama Boye to pour him café Touba to go, adds: Children nowadays, they watch movies and want to live like they do in the West. But this is not the West. This is Senegal.

▽ ▲ ▽

The next morning is Tamkharit, the day that commemorates the anniversary of the murder of the Prophet Muhammad's grandson Imam Hussein ibn Ali during the Battle of Karbala. Arabs call it Ashura, the Tenth: the tenth day of Muharram, the first month of the Islamic New Year. Fishermen consider this day a year's beginning. First guest of the day: a toad. He appears on the narrow patch of floor of my rental room and sings happy songs of wet kingdoms.

The rainy season should have been over a month ago. But this year it arrived two months late and now it refuses to end. Silver rain pours on the Petite Côte, on pirogues beached and anchored, darkens shell middens, drenches crews at sea. Farmers who already have harvested their crops and store them traditionally, unsheltered in the open, are in trouble.

By midmorning the blood of sheep slaughtered in holiday sacrifice coagulates in deep browngreen puddles of rainwater, and in

Joal's two outdoor markets housewives tiptoe around soggy refuse to buy millet, onions, tomato paste, margarine, and milk for the holiday feast: oily homemade millet couscous soaked in milk and served on gigantic communal tin platters with a sauce of meat or onions. Evening alleys fill with trick-or-treating children. *Oupas*, blacksmiths, market porters, students, servant girls. Crossdressed, in whiteface and makeup. In the tentative light of sparse streetlamps they bang on plastic buckets and tin plates and dance on wet sand demanding millet and coins, beautiful pagan dances much older than Imam Ali or Islam. Adults watch from thresholds, from plastic armchairs and low wooden stools pulled into alleyways, clap, laugh. Later, the entire Muslim coast all the way to Cameroon bends over traditional Tamkharit dinners.

The thirty-eight members of the Souaré household eat together under a waxing three-quarter moon cottonwooled in orange cloud. Ousmane is there, grimy and disgruntled after a day at sea. He never got up the nerve the night before to speak to his dad about returning to school. And in the morning, when it rained and the whole world was a gray cloud, Ndongo roused him and ordered him to go fishing. And that was that.

▽ ▲ ▽

The day after Tamkharit the fishermen stay home, digest last night's meal, pick at leftovers. All morning the boats nuzzle the shore: the tide is going out. A black sea, an iron sea. The horizon is emerald against the dark gray sky. The world is motionless.

A white heron stands on the stern of an anchored pirogue. Then it lifts off, rises against the green and the gray. Its flight is the only movement for miles, for latitudes.

Only at night do clouds part, let the moon roll in.

▽ ▲ ▽

Oh, Ndongo says. When I don't go to sea my body feels weird. It feels restless.

He is ashore again to monitor the work on the new pirogue. Master Ndoye may be the expert, but it is Ndongo who will pilot the boat, so he sticks around while his halfbrother Maguette takes the *Sakhari Souaré* fishing. He watches the shipwright butt planks that are not long enough with pieces he chops closely to fit. Helps him feather smaller cracks with splines, with wood chips, with flotsam. Ndongo and I vise ends of long mahogany boards between our shins as Master Ndoye saws or axes through the middle.

Often, though, Ndongo will just stand there, turn that faraway gaze to the sea as it becomes turquoise then green then black then golden. Ndongo. Ndongo! He is gone. I think he lifts out of his body like a genie and goes off to skim the surface, watch for the whispered evanescence of change as fish schools pass just below, the miniature serial explosions of mullet jumping, mermaids and sea spirits driving sardinella back and forth.

I understand the addiction. Within a month of arrival in Joal I find myself making daily rounds of calls to the pirogue captains

I know, and to ones I don't but whose phone numbers I have procured from friends. I ask when they are going to sea next. I set up rotating schedules: fourteen hours on a gillnetter, rest, sixteen hours on a purse seiner, rest, a day on a murex boat, repeat. My eyes adjust to the immensity of the ocean's volume, my hips and knees to its multifaceted angularity. Onboard I forget to care about decimated fisheries, about my contribution to broken ecosystems, about pirogues skimming the rim of catastrophe. Everything screams to a point at the single insatiable fixation: to cast and haul, again and again. The ocean bewitches, reveals the ancient predator in me.

The ocean, an old fisherman tells me, lays bare the avarice of man.

▽ ▲ ▽

A dozen times, while Ndongo pines for open sea, I plead myself aboard a purse seiner that belongs to my next-door neighbor, Captain Mamour Ndiaye. He lives in a small house right on the beach in the very center of Joal. When his pirogue is at anchor he can see her through the front door. Six dark bedrooms fan out from a long and narrow roofless hallway like the pinnate leaves of the benzoil tree that gives the house afternoon shade. The house and the hallway are painted electric blue, cobalt, indigo; being inside makes you feel comfortably submerged. The structure is concrete mixed with clamshells and where the paint is chipped it exposes the shells, the same *Senilia senilis* that make up the Isle of Fadiouth. The hallway dead-ends at an apse stenciled with larger-than-life portraits of Serigne Mouhamadou Fallou Mbacké and Serigne Abdou Khadre Mbacké, caliphs of the Mouride Sufi brotherhood. When Mamour is home he usually sits in a molded plastic chair at the end of the hallway, beneath the apse, his back to the stern caliphs, his eyes on the sea, a small towel tied around his waist. A narrow stripe of graying hair runs up his muscular belly. He is forty-five.

Mamour lives in the house with his second wife, Yacine Diop, their two children, his two teenage sons from his first marriage, and his perpetually rotating crew. Before they move on, deckies write their phone numbers in chalk on the indigo hallway walls. They sign the phone numbers with misspelled names. One has signed with an X. That is fine: the captain remembers who it was. The first time I ask to go to sea aboard his purse seiner he just shrugs and smiles. Anyone can come as long as they work and don't get in the way. Besides, he is stoned. Shrugging and smiling come easiest.

Mamour's pirogue is the *Mansor Sakho*: sixty-nine feet, twenty crew, a sixty-horsepower outboard. Except for the gunwales, which were once painted red, she is turquoise inside and out. Turquoise is the color of all Mamour's previous pirogues, and the pirogues his father and uncles once sailed in Mbour. The color sometimes of the sea and of the sky above the sea. The color to ward off evil spirits. One of the crew, Fily Sylla, says the color

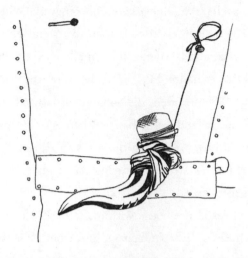

guarantees that the pirogue returns home safely and full of fish. Fily goes fishing in a blue and turquoise checkered tee shirt and blue swimming trunks for the same reason. He also wears a gris-gris belt around his waist. Everyone aboard wears gris-gris, including the pirogue. A ram's horn wrapped in cloth hangs inside her bow. From the footrope of her black multifilament net dangle leather and plastic pouches with sanctified Koranic verses. The net is more than a mile long, sequined with fish scales from catches past. Its vertical wall is ten fathoms deep. The crew say it can wrap ten tons of fish at a haul. They have never hauled that much fish at once.

The fishermen wade to the pirogue single file through the green surf of dawn holding plastic bags with their mess high above their heads. They shinny up the boomkin and into the

stern, run up the gunwales to the net hold amidships, and instantly settle upon the folded net to scarf down their breakfasts.
Entire baguettes split lengthwise and smeared with chocolate
spread. Tiny plastic bags with runny peanut butter: chew off a
corner and suck the contents out. Po'boys with murex or shrimp
drowned in palm oil, with beans and spaghetti, with stewed onions, with fish and french fries and hardboiled eggs. Fily, who is
nineteen and is training to become a professional wrestler, arranges his thunderous body on the net and methodically devours
two po'boys with shrimp, beans, spaghetti, onions, boiled potatoes, and eggs all mixed together and topped with mayonnaise.
My son is also nineteen, also voracious. It occurs to me that I miss
cooking for him. Fily notices my breakfast—a hardboiled egg, a
small green apple, a piece of baguette—and my stare.

Anna! Have some of my breakfast!

Oh no. I just want to watch. Thank you, though.

The food is gone before Mamour has finished rigging the fuel
line to the outboard. An *oupa* ducks into a hold and comes up
with a brazier made of a steel car wheel filled with concrete. He
douses two handfuls of charcoal in motor fuel and sets them
ablaze to start a pot of strong sweet tea. In the morning twilight
the flame aboard a sailing boat looks ceremonial, sacred. Mamour
steers westward to a fishing ground twenty miles offshore. This
will take a while. Men sprawl on the net, daydream, talk.

Of all the places I've been I like Saint-Louis the best.

Why?

They have nice girls.

Eh? Come on now, spill it out!

Do you have a girl in Saint-Louis?

He has a girl in every port!

I don't! But one time we went fishing to Mauritania and we stopped in Saint-Louis to refuel and pick up provisions and I really liked it there.

But the sea is rough there.

Oh, man, that's man's sea up there. You have to have a really good captain to sail to Mauritania from Saint-Louis.

Amen amen amen.

Beam sea. The scarlet crust of sunup over twelve-foot swells. Backlit, men bob atop the water, fall in and out of sleep, refill and pass around shot glasses of foamy tea. A largeheaded fisherman everyone calls Hôpital is passed out facedown on the net. In the purpling sky above, four black egrets and one white.

Lie down on the net. Prop your shoulders against the pirogue's blue ceiling to squint at the rising sun. With your upper back feel the swells beat against the hull. That soft ceaseless knocking, a metronome that pulses upon three-quarters of the world. Or maybe a countdown, begun four billion years back, after a rainy season that had lasted millions of years and that had rained an ocean covering the whole of Hadean Earth. What was it like after that cloud cover thinned, lifted, and the sun shone upon the water for the very first time?

Done with the tea, the men fish out two handfuls of spiny

murex shells from the bilge. Ancient Phoenicians—a coastal people who rarely ventured inland beyond ports and who created the world's first phonemic alphabet that eventually evolved into most modern scripts—made dye from its slimy mauve mucus; the dye, Tyrian or royal purple, was used for ceremonial and regal garments. The biblical blue of the robes the high priest of the Temple of Jerusalem wore may have come from murex snails. Hellenic snails: Aristotle gave the predatory mollusk its name in the fourth century B.C. The ones in the bilge are yesterday's bycatch, today's tabnabs. The fishermen balance them on the smoldering coals of the brazier.

The shells blacken. The men pick them off the coals, smash them against the gunwales, thumb out the rubbery flesh, lean overboard to rinse it in seawater. Fily hands me one. Onshore you buy fresh murex at the harbor already shelled, and the women who clean it pile the broken exoskeletons in two reeking heaps considerately downwind from the port trade. Murex sauce is a bistro staple; on the afternoons when I help my landlady with kitchen prep for the bistro she runs on Boulevard Jean Baptiste Collin, I chop several pounds of the boiled gristly mollusk into tiny cubes that stain my fingers lavender and violet before she boils them again in oily turmeric sauce until the meat is bright yellow and tastes like oil-soaked rubber. Fishermen put this in their po'boys; my landlady packs murex sauce po'boys for my tabnabs and asks me to bring back fish for lunch, as she would her husband if he were still a fisherman. The grilled gastropod

Fily gives me is entirely different: tubular, tender, pale pink, slightly charred on one side. It tastes sweet, salty, smoky all at once, like the mother sea.

The *Mansor Sakho* casts four times. The net slips overboard to port and the pirogue circles counterclockwise until the yellow floats of the seine line up in a broad hoop. Then the men grab the cinchline strung through the rusted steel rings at the bottom of the net and begin to haul.

A purse seine's cinchline is three inches thick. It tightens the bottom of the net like a drawstring, trapping the catch inside. You haul this line against the pull of the net, the drag of the current, the line's own waterlogged weight. This work is so hard the fishermen fall backward after each pull. Their hands are more calloused then the soles of my feet. I bail bilgefuls of seawater mixed with their sweat.

The fishermen ululate and knock into one another and swear and sing up the fish:

Haul like a madman!—Yeah!—Work like a donkey!—Yeah!—Work like a lion!—Hey!—Work, motherfucker!—Hey!—Don't be lazy!—And haul it haul it haul it yeah!

Their favorite rounds. In the stern, Mamour empties two sandbags into the sea to muddle the water and disorient the fish, stomps on the burden boards. The men's shrieking shanty is no longer workmanlike but ecstatic, orgasmic almost, dissolving into a shouted barrage of encouragements and nonsensical oaths—

Come on, baby!

Last night I fucked my girlfriend, I was hard all night!

Eh, *¿que paso?*

Eh, take no pity on that net!

Heave-ho!

—then gathering once more into rhythmic song until the net is cinched at last and someone ties the cinchline to the turquoise shapeless figurehead axed out of a redwood log and the men fall back into the holds, collapse onto one another, breathe.

After a few minutes the crew slowly disentangle, stand up, take long drinks of water from one of the two large jerrycans the *Mansor Sakho* carries aboard. Then they strip down to their skivvies and douse themselves with seawater from the bailing cans made out of containers that once held cooking oil, and some jump overboard squealing with pleasure and some stand on the starboard gunwale pissing downwind, away from the swimmers and the net. Eventually all return to midships, grab their mess bags from the stern. They are hungry again. They mix drinking water with the homemade millet couscous women sell along the shore before sunrise. The couscous is soursmelling and gritty like wet cement. Some add powdered milk and sugar. Hôpital mixes his with seawater. When he began to fish twenty-three years ago he would give unsolicited medical advice, earning his nickname; now he talks little, and when he is not hauling net he smokes pot or eats or sleeps. The crew roll joints. Mamour is on his fifth. He does not pass them, smokes alone. Aphasic by now, he tosses his chin to signal the crew, and they get up and haul net. Ten fathoms of mystery twinkle below.

Men sing.

I know Muhammad—work like a donkey—there's a woman at the *mbaar*—there's a white woman in the boat—there's a white woman in the net—a girl can't refuse a man—I've got many mouths to feed . . .

A sole sardine, no larger than a palm, floats white belly-up to the surface. Men stop singing, just haul, exhale loudly as they pull on the floatline. It takes a crew of twenty men half an hour to haul a mile-long seine.

Wait for it.

When the black mass of the seine emerges in full it holds no sardines. A few halfbeaks. Several murex shells, pink like tongue. Either the *Mansor Sakho* missed the school entirely or else the fish were so small they twisted right through the fine mesh. The crew fall back down on the net. More joints. More snacks. The swells have turned into fast chop and the *oupa*, a thirteen-year-old named Adama, is sick over the starboard gunwale. Adama is a village boy, a farmboy. This is his third day at sea.

When I first went to sea I was also seasick, says Mamour.

In some seas even the most experienced fishermen are seasick, says Hôpital.

It's the fish smell, says Pa Pape Ndiaye, Mamour's tiny and toothless first mate.

What fish smell, old man? There's no fish.

This kind of chop brings fish, Mamour says.

On her third cast of the day the *Mansor Sakho* hauls a few boxes of round sardinella. In her wake the pearly plumes of broken fish scales swirl like nail polish and the bail is dark with fish blood. A brick-red seahorse, a rescue from the seine, wraps around my wrist and fingers needily, forcefully, like an infant.

⋎ ⋀ ⋎

The sun falls toward a white western sea. The desperate boat pivots and casts her net two miles inside the sanctuary off Joal's coast.

Make it fast, boys, we're not supposed to be here! Mamour tells the crew.

They sing under their breath now. After they have cinched the seine they gather to port and lean over the gunwale and silently watch. Divining the haul.

Nothing.

The pirogue speeds to her anchorage. The subdued crew eat leftover couscous, drink more tea, roll more joints.

If we see a sea turtle we will catch it and sell it, says Hôpital.

No, man. It's illegal to catch sea turtles.

⋎ ⋀ ⋎

At the harbor the bedlam of fishwives and porters briefly encircles the *Mansor Sakho*. While the captain negotiates the fish price a horsecart driver whips Pa Pape Ndiaye in the nuts with a riding crop. The old man doubles over, hissing promises of revenge, but no one pays much attention to the altercation, and when I ask him what had brought it on he just smiles. The sun sets and the sea pales to a yellowish mother-of-pearl, and the wind suddenly blows cold. In the dying sky, the first swallows of the season somersault in hunt.

▽ ▲ ▽

N oon at the Souarés' dry dock. Ever the bargain hunter, Amadou has procured some cheap mahogany from a friend. The boards have been sitting on the beach in the sun for months. They are narrow and dry, infested with ants. The carpenter kerfs one anyway, dowels it onto the port garboard, slings a ratchet strap over it and the starboard, cranks the ratchet. The dry board snaps. Master Ndoye sucks his gums and retreats to the *mbaar* to pray the *Zuhr*. Amadou does not show he has noticed, leads the prayer.

Cheap old fart, Ndongo mutters.

He orders Ousmane inside the boat, tells him to collect loose nails and dowels and sort them by size. The boat is propped up on three palm trunks, a sandbag, and, at the bow, two old boards from some other broken pirogue, dug into the beach at an angle and nailed at their vertex to the keel as a support.

With his right pinkie Ndongo stirs a pinch of yellow powder into a shot glass of tepid water. Ground mimosa bark, against stomachache and Satan. Also against tetanus: there are many rusty nails about, and no one is wearing shoes. You never do inside a boat, just as you never wear shoes inside a house or a mosque. If you apply a mimosa bark poultice to a cut, the wound will leave no scar. If you keep mimosa bark in your room, no vampires will enter. I take a sip.

▽ ▲ ▽

At six o'clock, three boys wearing bluejeans and blue tee shirts scramble into the *Mama Woly Thior*, a hundred-and-thirty-foot beached pirogue awaiting a paint job between the tideline and Mbaar Kanené. They are brothers; the oldest is ten. They tie two lengths of line three inches thick to the purse seiner's center thwarts, chuck the loose ends over to port, rappel down. They knot thick figure eights at the bottom of the lines, for seats. Then two of them straddle the knots and, coordinating their start times with the focus and seriousness of children at play, they begin to swing.

I watch.

Then I can no longer watch.

May I?

Of course!

I hike up my skirt and mount one of the lines. That sweet delay in the diaphragm, the nag of the ribcage rushing ahead of the heart. That pelagic rocking, that imitated flight, that odd momentary deafness that comes with each forward thrust: sensations that seem remembered, recovered almost, from way before the swings of my childhood. Like the recollection of Atlantis—the mysterious sunken continent that, had it ever been real, would have been what we now know as the Mid-Atlantic Ridge, under-water for at least sixty million years and so able to exist only in our pre-memory, cellular memory. The impression of being rocked by the ocean.

I swing. The world ebbs and flows, flips, the pink glow of sunset flashes on a seagull's wing above, below. The Souarés' unfinished pirogue swings in her dry dock upon the oscillating sand. Out of the corner of my eye I see Daouda Sarr's beached boat, the *Stacko Mbacké*: it is full of kids and they jostle for the bowsprit, play king of the boat, yell: My boat my boat my boat my boat! The shore is ravenously, outrageously alive. The kings of the boat laugh. The boys on the rope swing laugh. I laugh. I am a child: on the ocean we all are, forever suspended on its timeless, place-less swing.

▽ ▲ ▽

The storm that destroyed the Souarés' pirogue also broke two of the four flagpoles that displayed coastal warning flags in Joal. Now one advisory flag flies from the veranda of the little green seaside mosque in the center of town. The mosque has no name, but people call it Joalis Mosque, after the nearest landmark, the nightclub Joalis, just down the block. Our Lady of the Disco.

Inside the veranda there are benches, and from the ceiling hangs a small section of a purse seine stuffed with teapots, tea glasses, prayer rugs. Outside, near the painted pirogue boards stuck into the sand to support neighborhood laundry lines, is a small smithy where two teenage boys forge kedges and cuttlefish traps out of rebar. Joal's harbormaster, Ibrahima Samb, who lives nearby, passes the blacksmiths twice daily to hoist the Joalis Mosque flag himself after receiving marine forecasts from the state meteorological service in Dakar. Green, yellow, red. Harbormaster Samb's younger brother, a fisherman, perished at sea two years ago. That was before the flags.

The other flag flies on the beach behind the town hospital, by the southernmost town *mbaar*, the one called Mbaar Sarrené, where few pirogues are moored and where family homes give way to the sprawling walled villas of white vacationers from Europe. It is hitched to an electric pole. Harbormaster Samb is not sure who flies that flag; he forwards the weather advisory, by text message, to a few fishermen who live around there, but the flags are rarely in sync. Anyway, most fishermen rely on the knowledge of weather patterns and lunar cycles they have inherited from their fathers and mentors. They say such knowledge is more precise, and much more useful. Also, those who have television can get the official weather advisory after the evening news.

Neither the marine forecast nor the traditional knowledge predict the freak wave that one early November night hoists Vieux Sene's gillnetter, the *Cheikh Sadbou*, and slams her upside down into the hardpacked sand at low tide. Vieux arrives at the shore in midmorning to find her bow broken. He only just has repaired the pirogue after saving up for months. He put her in the water a few days before. He has not even taken her out to sea yet. It is a beautiful day, the sea is calm and mirrorlike, soft like a lover's belly. The world shimmers, rises and falls, gives and takes, turns.

▼ ▲ ▼

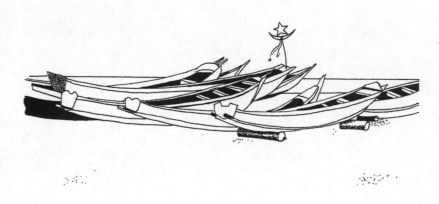

Four

The housegirl Fatou, harelipped, highstrung, and disliked, cleans mounds of sardinella and bonga shad for my landlady's bistro. The bistro stays open past midnight, is busiest late. Night after night on a low wooden stool in the outdoor kitchen outside my rental room she cleans. Fish blood runs down her knees and between her toes and sluices down the groutwork where the yard tilts toward the exterior wall of the compound painted with flamingos and sea turtles. The mural is invisible in the night, but even after dark clouds of blowflies swarm to Fatou's housework. The single fluorescent light tints the fish blue, the blood black. The girl wipes fish scales on her cornrows, croons an old folksong: A Serer goes to sea / goodbye, my love, I will be a fisherman / a Serer goes to sea / goodbye, my love, I will miss you.

Two blocks away great white egrets fold themselves for the night into the tallest branches of an old
baobab tree.

▽ ▲ ▽

Morning rushes in with a sheen of birds. At the northwest tip of
the Isle of Fadiouth a horsecart squishes through a slurry of pig
shit and seashell and lumbers up a wooden bridge. It carries one
passenger.

The cart rattles past the white shell mound of the cemetery
and down a muddy laterite road that runs through the mangroves.
They say hyenas live in the mangroves now that the bush is rav-
aged by systemic drought and man. No hyenas come out to greet
the horsecart, but at its approach a hundred weavers explode out
of the sole acacia tree that grows among the mangroves.

The cart's passenger is eighty-four years old, wilted and small,
in a white skullcap, a soiled white boubou down to his knees,
white loose cotton trousers, and black foam flipflops with white
stripes. The stubble on his face, too, is white. He is Simon Ndiaré
Ndiaye, King of the Sea. He is headed away from the coast, to the
bush, to the house of termites. He is carrying a plastic bag full of
millet.

The road splits and curves and after an hour or so the cart is
out of the mudflats. The land here is very dry and red. There are
thick baobab trees, tall doum palms, soggy bales of millet straw,
termite mounds. At a spot only he knows, a spot his maternal

grandfather taught him when he was a child, King of the Sea dismounts and shuffles toward the mounds. There, he pours the millet on the ground and speaks to the termites.

Termites, he says. His voice is a croak, a rasp. Termites. You have to travel far to find millet. But today I got you this millet and brought it close to your home. In return I want you to bring fish close to the fishermen. I leave you this millet here and I want you to send fish to the sea. I am buying your service. It is a fair exchange.

Termites are like humans. They populate every continent except Antarctica. They often occupy the same mounds for centuries, though termite queens rarely live longer than fifty years. Even after the insects leave, their cemented structures remain, outlandish sandcastles with minarets and spires, some as tall as granaries, some shaped like tombstones and mysteriously oriented north to south. One mound, in the Congo, has been carbon-dated to two thousand and two hundred years. As old as Paris and Bratislava, as old as Eratosthenes's calculation of the circumference of the Earth. People in Southeast Asia come to termite mounds to pray for health and luck, Aboriginal Australians use them for witchcraft, Hindus bedeck them into shrines. They are expiatory temples for generations of humans all over the world, Sagrada Famílias of the bush.

After making his plea, King of the Sea collects some soil from the termite mounds, puts it in his plastic bag, shambles back to the horsecart, returns to Fadiouth. At the small island market he buys catfish, sardine, ray, shark, monkfish, any other kind of fish on sale, one of each, and takes them to the small adobe house that he shares with his only wife and that he has decorated with a reproduction of Leonardo da Vinci's *Last Supper.* He cuts off the tail fins and divides the soil from the termite mounds into two parts. He mixes the fish tails with one part of the soil and waits for low tide. Then he walks to the ocean. He walks slowly because he can barely unbend.

He puts the soil he has mixed with the fish tails in the water. He puts the rest of the soil at the wrackline so the sea can take it when high tide comes: seconds, dessert. Then he wades into the water himself.

King of the Sea must always wear white and never spend a night outside Fadiouth. He is elected for life by a congress of elders of the Diakhanora, a vast matrilineal clan of keepers of the sea who choose the king from among Diakhanora men. Centuries ago the Diakhanora may have been fishermen; now they are farmers, engineers, civil servants, bus drivers, teachers. After the death of the previous King of the Sea, a Diakhanora delegation came from Dakar and told Simon it was his turn.

Simon Ndiaré Ndiaye said no. He is Christian. One of his sons is a Catholic priest in Joal. King of the Sea is a pagan tradition, it goes against his faith. For three years, the sea had no king.

It was his priest son who changed the old man's mind. He said this:

If you become King of the Sea and say a special prayer and fish come, they won't be just for you, not just for Joal and Fadiouth, but for all of the sea, all the fishermen, and all the people in the world who depend on these fish. It is not a sin.

So Simon agreed. Now he must ask the termites to calm the sea when it is rowdy, make it plentiful when it is empty. In exchange for donations of fish, money, and fortified red wine he gives fishermen soil from the termite mounds, to sprinkle in their nets, stash inside their sinkers, hide inside their pirogues, attract fish. He is passing on his magical knowledge to his matrilineal cousins. If there is another King of the Sea in the world he has never heard of him.

After his bath in the ocean Simon prays again. He asks Jesus Christ to help all the fishermen. He reminds Christ that He Himself has been a fisherman and that He once helped fishermen fill their nets in the Sea of Galilee. Simon reasons that He can help fishermen fill their nets again. Amen.

▽ ▲ ▽

Around the same time, in a large house on the northeast edge of Joal, where pale sand dunes grow out of an iridescent sludge of rotting rainwater, the sorcerer Adama Sidy begins to have visions. Of a sea troubled, an angry sea. Of sacrifices of sweet millet *lakh* and *ceebu jën*, performed by the town's fishermen under his supervision. The visions persist daily.

The sorcerer receives me in his bedroom. Its furniture is outsize. A huge wardrobe, a massive matrimonial bed, stacks and stacks of enameled steel cooking pots. He directs me to one of the

two big ugly upholstered armchairs, then lies down on the floor
to talk. He is wearing only green polyester gym pants. A tall man
in his middle age. His torso looks soft, puffy almost: he is not a
fisherman. He is worrying something in his mouth, a piece of
kola nut, or a rock. A fish bone maybe. His room smells like fish.
Everything in Joal smells like fish, even my pillow.

What he tells me is vague, abstract. Visions of troubles. Visions of sacrifice. Making peace with the sea. God willing. After
some time he stops talking and recedes into a smile. His tongue
works around that thing in his mouth. As if there is no language
yet for what he knows.

After the feast of Tamkharit, when Harbormaster Samb crosses
Boulevard Jean Baptiste Collin and arrives at Adama's house, the
sorcerer is expecting him.

▽ ▲ ▽

Anna. We are cooking the food. At seaside of the harbor.
Come.

The harbormaster speaks choppy, assertive English. He is large
with large hands, most fingernails rotten. The ones that are not
are very long and elegantly manicured. He favors gray robes and
white leather babouche slippers. He keeps track of things: weather
forecasts and boating accidents, pirogues flagged to Joal and their
catch, sacrifices to the sea.

At nine-thirty in the morning the harbor is a mild hum, a
slow carousel of vendors selling peanuts and café Touba, of mid-

dlemen on their cellphones. A few boats roll in shoreline slop, moored to makeshift bollards of palm trunks, of driftwood, of beached pirogues. On the sand dark with fish blood and boat fuel and manure, boys unload a cartful of blue and white molded plastic chairs that have numbers handpainted on their backs, to keep track of the loaners. Some of these chairs come from my landlord's house. The calm ocean is black to slate gray to pale green where it meets the sand, and there now Adama Sidy stands in a striped brown boubou and a baseball cap, with a shaggy miswak stick between his teeth. He is holding a calabash in his right hand and a bottle of fortified red wine in his left. He stares at the variegated sea. Calculating something. Or remembering. Having another vision maybe. Then he turns his back on the water and strides to the harbor building. There, on a terrace under the northern half of the seafacing tin awning, two dozen fishwives are preparing the sacrificial feast.

A hundred pounds of millet to boil into runny *lakh* porridge, with almost as much sweet sauce of peanut butter and yogurt. A hundred pounds of onions to stew into a relish. Several hundred bonga shad: the fish will return to the sea deepfried to a lacy crisp. A hundred pounds of rice. The sea must be hungry. All the provisions are courtesy of the harbor, purchased by Harbormaster Samb with the money from the harbor's treasury.

The women work in circles: a peanut sauce mixing circle, a fish cleaning circle, an onion peeling circle, a rice sifting circle. In mermaid dresses and matching headwraps printed with fish, with butterflies, with politicians and saints and caliphs and birds and shrimp. Arranged on woven plastic mats like huge flower corolla. They whisk, peel, cut, gossip, joke, swat at flies. From time to time, one or two of the older fishwives rise slowly and shuffle over to check on the *lakh* that is boiling in two enormous cast-iron cauldrons balanced on log fires lit right on the concrete floor. Names are etched into the lids and bellies of the cauldrons: MATY-KANE. MAIMOUNA DIOKH. They are so large you can cook a whole calf in each. They have personalities; they deserve names. The *lakh* thickens, spits hot amber bubbles. The women stir it with blackened shovels they hold with both hands. Witches back-lit by the sea, half submerged in steam, performing the oldest alchemy. When their husbands are angry and withholding, do they cook for them as well?

The day grows hotter and the ocean turns bluegray, minutely speckled with barely perceptible wind. A pelican sits on it. Old men arrive, file onto the terrace through the doors of the harbor building tracing dark puddles of fishrot. More men walk up the stairs from the beach. They sit in the shade of the awning at the southern end of the terrace, separate from the women. The harbormaster shuttles between the men and the women, checks his wristwatch, consults with the sorcerer in whispers. He switches to French-inflected English to explain:

We wanted to kill cow. But this year Adama Sidy—the fetish man—said cow is not good sacrifice. This year we do *lakh*, white rice, and fish. It is *une* prayer. Really God decides. But we hope for positive results.

By half past ten, two hundred or more men have gathered, mostly old fishermen, and two or three dozen *talibé* boys. They turn their backs on the sea and face the wall of the harbor building. The wall is chipped blue, smeared with months-old fish blood. An altar. They intone the Koran, kneel in communal invocation. Someone passes around a tin platter with hard Mauritian dates. The women just keep working. Their cooking is their prayer.

It was a woman's cooking that tricked Ndiadian Ndiaye into becoming the first ruler of the Wolof. After the death of his father, the Almoravid chieftain Abou Bakr ibn Umar ibn Ibrahim ibn Turgut, who had come south from the Sahara and settled at the headwaters of the Senegal River in the eleventh century, Ndiadian Ndiaye's widowed mother, the Fulani princess Fatoumata Sall, followed her late husband's will and married their servant. Prissy and indignant at his mother's remarriage, Ndiadian Ndiaye threw himself into the river and remained stubbornly afloat for seven years until he overheard a group of child fishers quarrelling over their catch and stepped in. Hearing of Ndiadian Ndiaye's wise counsel, local adults caught him with fishnets, hauled him ashore, and begged him, this African Perseus, to become their ruler. Reluctant to put down roots, Ndiadian Ndiaye decided to outwit the villagers by feigning muteness. Until an astute young woman came out with a cooking pot and two stones, set up this lopsided kitchen in front of the prisoner, and pretended to try to cook.

The bipod did not work, of course: it was not supposed to. The pot kept slipping off into the fire. Ndiadian Ndiaye watched until at last his patience grew so thin he could no longer hold his tongue. *Wallahi*, woman, use three stones! he said. And, realizing he had spoken, gave up and agreed to become the village king, the first king of the Jolof in the land of the Wolof.

And it remains so: Water transports and converts; women hoodwink men into settling down by feigning weakness; when women work, men sit around and give advice unbidden; and, since even settled men are rarely home long enough, it falls to women to tend to domestic magic.

▽ ▲ ▽

The ocean has Mami Wata and hundreds of lesser spirits, but anyone can have a protector genie. To procure one, you find a wooden post in your house, or plant one in the dirt, or select a particular tree, and every morning you pour some beer or milk at its base. After a few years you begin to feel a presence. Your genie has arrived. Now you have to take care of it, offer it sweets, whisper it prayers.

Genii repay in kind. When Vieux Sene's mother was younger, each time she would give birth a snake would appear in the rafters of the house and watch. It was the family protector genie. Vieux has not seen the genie snake in years, not since his mother became too old to have children. Ndongo's mother, Fatou Diop Diagne, offers the genie widow of her great-grandfather *lakh* and milk whenever a girl child is born in the family, and in return the genie protects the girl from illness. Though protector genii prefer to liaise through women, on occasion a genie may choose a man to take care of it. Daouda Sarr says that in Palmarin there is a man whose grandmother was a caretaker for several protector genii. After the woman died the genii decided that her grandson would take her place, even though he was working in a different town and had no intention to return to Palmarin. So the genii made him very sick, forcing him to come to Palmarin to recuperate among family. When he arrived, his arms suddenly became very weak, so he could not go back to work, could not leave the village, had to stay and take care of the genii. Now he has gone a little bit mad.

On the day of the sacrifice at the harbor Fatou Diop Diagne is in Dakar selling shrimp. She does not attend the ceremony; none of my fishermen friends do. Daouda Sarr tends to his sheep. Ndongo spends the day helping Master Ndoye and mending, with

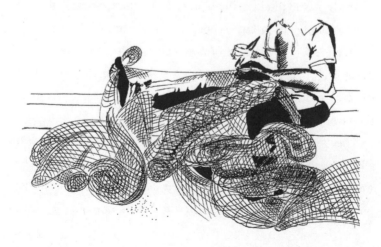

Vieux Sene's help, a thirty-millimeter net, in anticipation of larger sardines, while Amadou Souaré, Pa Yagmar Kane, Pa Bara Diop, and Pa Ousmane Sall keep an eye on the working men, kvetch at the *mbaar*. Mamour Ndiaye goes to sea aboard the *Mansor Sakho*; he catches little.

I cannot spot Lamine Ndong, the *chef du village,* at the harbor. When I ask him about it later he says:

Perhaps I was there, perhaps I was not. I am eighty-four. I have troubles of memory.

▽ ▲ ▽

The prayer is over at quarter past eleven. The supplicants turn their hands palm upward in request of a blessing. A gift, a bit of magic. Fish. They draw their fingers down their faces, seal their covenant with the merciful and omnipotent God.

With plastic pitchers the women ladle the *lakh* into fifty aluminum basins, each large enough to bathe in, pour the peanut sauce on top. The offering of *lakh* comes before the *ceebu jën* because it is sugary and the sea has a sweet tooth. If you sacrifice the *lakh* and the rice and fish at the same time the sea will reject the savory oblation.

They serve the sea first. Two *talibé* boys and a fishwife pick up a basin each and walk slowly and solemnly down the steps. They wade waist-deep into the water, their clothes now billowed, now plastered skintight by waves, tilt the basins into the limegreen surf, and dip the platters in the water to rinse them. Instantly there comes a rush, a shouting of directions and orders, and the townfolk on the terrace cluster around the remaining platters, the leftovers of the genii feast. They stand and squat and sit in mingled and fluid groups of five or six and dip their fingers in the runny cereal and with these stained fingers and palms wave at one another, beckon: Come eat with us! Eat with us! Eat here!

Come eat! I squat next to four fishwives. The *lakh* is visceral on my fingers, like the insides of something holy or alive. It is delicious. The millet is silky sweet, and there is the gentle smoky tang of the peanut sauce and the sour creaminess of yogurt.

After the adults finish eating, the *talibé* lick the basins clean. Forever hungry growing boys. They spend their days running in the streets in prankish packs, and they will be ravenous again by the time rice and fish are served, after the Zuhr.

▽ ▲ ▽

At noon exactly Adama Sidy leads a procession to the tideline. He wades ankle-deep into the surf and turns the uncorked wine bottle upside down. The dark red pours into the green. He tosses underhand into the sea the bottle, then the cork. Bends down and scoops a calabash full of sanctified harbor water.

All of a sudden the crowd behind him begins to clap. Stomp. Ululate. Then a fishwife rips off her headdress and blouse and runs into the water topless and whooping. Another. Ten, twenty, fifty men and women and boys run and wade into the sea, some stripping and some not, staggering and falling down like drunks, like lunatics, diving, clapping, laughing, lifting their palms to the sky, singing and speaking in tongues, clomping through the water in euphoria. They come out and dip their fingers in the calabash the sorcerer holds out to them, run the fingers across their faces, and proffer to the fetish man plastic bags and cupped palms and bonnets and baseball caps and fedoras: pour more please, more, more holy water to take home to lave themselves and their children and their relatives and neighbors. They run once more into the hallowed surf, fall in again, again.

I recognize this rapture. I have read about it in a book. Martin Klein's description of that spontaneous cleansing of the freed slaves in Saint-Louis almost two hundred years earlier: This is what that looked like. This is what that was. A baptism. A ritual as old as man's life by the sea.

I think: If I were the ocean I would barf up some sardines.

☶ ☶ ☶

In the net hold of the *Mansor Sakho* fishermen chow down on their po'boys while Captain Mamour Ndiaye, in rolled-up gym pants and a black tanktop printed with neon-green marijuana leaves, prepares the pirogue for a day at sea. He wets a branch of sabara tree in seawater and whips the boat with it. He whips the gunwales and the bow. Inside the chain locker. Inside the net hold. The net itself. He grins and makes as if to whip Hôpital, who is asleep upon the net. Spotted, glaucous leaves fly.

Sabara, *Guiera senegalensis*, is a panacea. You use its bitter leaves to treat malaria, leprosy, cancer, venereal diseases, epilepsy and impotence, to fatten cows and to increase lactation among young mothers. You crush its leaves with tamarind pulp to serve as a condiment, and you smoke the dry leaves to treat respiratory ailments. An infusion of sabara leaves treats Guinea worm, protects newborn babies against black magic, and brings wealth. Its galls treat fowlpox and hypertension and its roots treat insomnia and dysentery. It prevents vomiting in small doses and induces it in large. In large doses it is hallucinogenic.

Mamour is giving the pirogue a no-holds-barred blessing because he is taking a day off today and is dispatching the *Mansor Sakho* with his younger brothers, Baye Djiby and Moustapha, as captain and first mate. He wants to make sure the boat is maximally protected for the trip.

Moustapha appreciates his eldest brother's thoughtfulness.

Makes us feel luckier, he says.

Moustapha is a melancholy man in his late thirties. He has lived in Spain for two years and speaks fluent Spanish and English in addition to the French and Wolof of the Petite Côte. For the first three months abroad he worked at a Nissan factory in Barcelona, on an assembly line. Then his contract ended and an economic crisis in Spain began, and there was no work. So he re-

turned: there is always work on his brother's boat. His wife and
toddler daughter live with his parents in Mbour, and he gets to
see them only once a week. That is hard. Life is so.

▿▵▿

C ast off. Baye Djiby orders an *oupa* to helm, setting course for
the pirogue's usual fishing grounds, twenty or thirty miles
east-southeast of Joal, then puts on headphones, pushes his baseball cap over his face, and lies down on the net. Violent smears of
orange and red vein the dawn horizon.

Men smoke joints, drink tea, chitchat. There was a match last
night, and the conversation turns to traditional wrestling, *laamb*,
a centuries-old pastime of fishers and farmers, Senegal's national
sport.

Laamb's objective is to lift the opponent off the ground and
toss him outside the sandy ring, or at least to hold his head or
back or both hands and knees to the sand. It allows strikes and
punches to the head and face. Televised matches pack stadiums
and are hours-long sideshow extravaganzas with bush doctors,
marabouts, musicians, sponsors, multicolored protective baths,
and eldritch rituals and dances of intimidation and swank. Most
fights last less than a minute. Often, a fight looks like two gar-
gantuan men crocheted in amulets slapping at each other like cats
for many long beats—then suddenly one is on the ground getting
his face pulped. Top-tier wrestlers train in Europe or North

America and make hundreds of thousands of dollars per fight. The most opulent seaside villas in Joal and all along the Petite Côte belong to laamb wrestlers. The most powerful marabouts are the ones in wrestlers' employ.

The Museum of African Arts, in Dakar, dedicates half of its exhibition space to laamb. There are some portraits of famous fighters. Serigne Ousmane Dia, known as Bombardier. Mamadou Sakho, known as Balla Gaye the Second or Double Less or the Lion of Guédiawaye. Mohammed Ndao, known as Tyson. Joal's own Yakhya Diop, known as Yékini, he of the famous uppercut. But mostly, it is an exhibit of gris-gris.

A knotted yarn rosary Alioune Ndour used in 1982 "to blow upon while reciting incantations to paralyze the adversary" and a white cotton rope dipped at measured intervals in something brown—blood?—Ndour wore that same year. Mamadou Ndong's armband of rope and driftwood, from 1977, which he wore "before going to fight or to ward off bad luck." Thick cotton belts basted together roughly with contrasting thread stuffed with something; anything. Rams' horns wrapped in red cloth. Scores of leather bracelets, anklets, knotted belts of homespun wool, coils of leather gris-gris twisted into cords many yards long. Cowrie shells sewn onto cotton, onto leather belts. A desiccated head of a rooster, its beak half-open, which Baye Gueye used in 1973 to discern his opponent's plan of attack.

I know this for a fact, Balla Gaye uses very strong magic to win, says young Issa Sow, who left his cattle in the heartland to become a fisherman, and whom everyone onboard calls Fulani.

Yeah. He uses bones of babies, says Fily Sylla, the aspiring wrestler.

Bullshit! says Modou Fall, the brother of Captain Mamour Ndiaye's wife. Where would he get bones of babies?

It's easy to get them here. You go to the cemetery, find the little graves, dig them up.

Yeah, I hear that's why after a match Balla Gaye gets on a pirogue to change so that no one sees him taking off his gris-gris.

Fily says:

I apprenticed with Eumeu Sène once. One time before a match he had us catch nine live dogs. Then he had them laid out in a row and stepped over each of them, to win.

Laamb, man.

Yeah, nasty stuff.

It's not the wrestlers competing; it's their marabouts' magic competing.

The *Mansor Sakho* herself is named after a marabout who once worked for Yékini. They say he betrayed Yékini and helped Balla Gaye the Second win the fabled Dakar match in 2012 that ended Yékini's two-decade reign as Senegal's champion. After Balla Gaye's stunning upset the marabout Mansor Sakho fell out of favor with Yékini. He remains Captain Mamour's friend.

For two years after that upset Balla Gaye the Second was the King of Arenas. He would strut into sportsplex rings trussed in amulets and wrapped in Koranic suras inscribed on homespun cloth in magic-spiked ink. Around him coaches would dance and marabouts would pour over his head potions that, it is said, contained lion hair and gazelle milk. He would stare his opponents in the face and mouth spells. Still, his title was shortlived: two years later, Bombardier pinned the champion to the same Dakar sand in thirty seconds; and the year following, in that very stadium, Eumeu Sène pulped his face less than a minute into the match people now call the Shock. Who knows if the winners had better form or stronger magic?

Do you believe in magic?

Sometimes. Do you?

No, man. I don't.

Bullshit! What about that time you had a bottle of holy water and sprayed it all over the boat?

That was for protection from the evil eye! It wasn't magic, it was real, because my parents gave it to me.

Magic, says Issa Fulani. He leans back on the net, closes his eyes, lets the ocean rock him. He keeps a sewing needle, for protection, next to a pack of cigarettes inside the sweatband of his faux suede hat. He misses to tears his cows and his young wife, who is not yet pregnant because he married her right before he headed off to sea. He is here because the Sahel has been in drought for years and cattle in the hinterlands no longer give enough milk to support a family.

They say if a pregnant woman sees someone eating something she cannot afford, and craves it, and at that moment of craving touches herself somewhere—on the belly, on a forearm—then when the baby is born the corresponding spot on the baby's body—the belly, the forearm—will have a spot, a birthmark. Issa's wife must want for nothing, especially when she is with his child.

▽ ▲ ▽

At eleven in the morning the *Mansor Sakho* approaches her fishing grounds. Other purse seiners are already about. Baye Djiby, the captain, who has been listening to the radio on his headphones since castoff, stands up. The crew rise also and stand on gunwales, on thwarts. Watch the sea.

Left arm tentatively up. Right arm. The surface puckers and streams, and my arms, too, involuntarily fly up—not so much an indication of fish or an alert as a greeting, an acknowledgment that we are passing one another in this ocean. Baye Djiby lies back down, adjusts his headphones. Too many other pirogues here. Hauling net is too exhausting to try and fail. He would rather cast once and haul a full seine, this way his men will be less tired. So he tells the helmsman full speed ahead, for now.

On the horizon, broad on the port bow, a large foreign trawler, flat and two-dimensional, like a shadow, a stage prop. A portent. We steer toward it, then north of it. It disappears. So do the pirogues and the fish schools.

The *Mansor Sakho* has used up a five-gallon jerrycan of fuel to get this far offshore. Baye Djiby whistles and an *oupa*, a new kid in his late teens, runs astern with a lit cigarette in his mouth. He unscrews the top off a full jerrycan, thumbs the piece of plastic bag that seals it, tosses it in the sea to starboard. Paisley plumes bloom on the green surface; my legs are splashed with gasoil mixture. He pulls the fuel line from the spent jerrycan and sinks it into the one he has just opened, tightens the lid, prances back amidships, puffing on his cigarette all the while.

Then, at one o'clock, the hands fly up: A school! A school! The captain whistles again and the crew cast the seine and cinch the purse line.

▽ ▲ ▽

M en haul net.
    Get 'er—get 'er—get 'er—get 'er!
Haul it!
Kill the fish!
Go in pairs, go in pairs!
Work like lions!
Work like a donkey!
Haul the motherfucking net, motherfucker, by the holy Koran!
The net is white with fish!

They haul and blaspheme and jeer and sing the hortatory chants they have heard on the many boats they crewed before up and down the coast, and they haul harder and whack the gunwales with burden boards, and three or four men dive into the water and beat it fiendishly, take out on the sea all the savage violence it does to them, mete out a merciless ceremonial punishment that at this very moment is replicated by the crews of thousands of other pirogues all along the seaboard.

Then you hear it.

Over the yelling and the whistling of the fishermen, over the idling of the motor, over the knocking and the splashing, you hear: fish pelting inside the surfacing net like rain.

When you haul a full seine of sardines out of the water the fish thrash so hard they spray the entire pirogue with water and seaweed and scales. When you tip the seine into the pirogue the fish sluice down into the holds with a deafening rustle like an enormous flock of birds awing. Passenger pigeons must have sounded like this as they passed over the American Midwest, before man shot them all out of the sky. In the boat the fish continue to throb for minutes.

On the way back to shore, Moustapha and I lie on the wet net side by side. Such a cloudless sky above us. Such a fickle sea below.

Do you think, I ask, that the sacrifice the old fishermen performed at the harbor the other day had anything to do with the haul?

I don't know. Maybe there were less fish before the sacrifice. It seems to me that after the sacrifice there have been more. But I don't know if it's because of the sacrifice. What I think is, Anna, it's because we *believe* in the sacrifice that we are getting more fish now.

But the sea is a picky eater. It chooses its sacrifice. Four days after the ceremony, it swallows Mansour "Action" Ndoye, a young fisherman who lives with his mother three blocks from my house. He drowns off the coast of Djifer, a port village by the Point of Sangomar, the genii gathering place, where fishermen from Joal occasionally spend the night and offload their catch, and where crazy rip currents tongue and suck the Saloum River's anabranches, assail the delta in an unbroken French kiss.

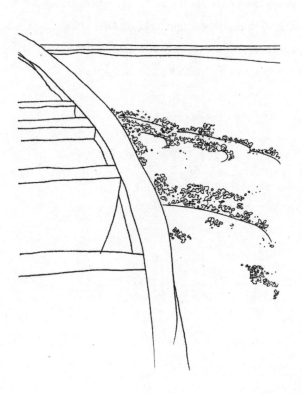

Five

A ction was an *oupa* on a pursenet pirogue that slipped her mooring during the night and drifted to sea. In the morning he swam out to fetch her.

They look for him all day. In gillnetters, in purse seiners, in trapsetters unsuited to the vigor of the outgoing riptide, the wooden boats daubed in primary colors like some maritime adaptation of clowns' wagons, the desperate crews lean overboard to stare at a sea that is all surface. Maybe suddenly the sun slants just so and in a boat's shadow the seabed shines up from ten fathoms below, clear and pale, speckled with colonies of mussels and clams and rocks. I have seen this happen. Then the boat turns, the ocean surface curtains, and the vision is gone.

They have no net large enough to dredge the sea.

▽ ▲ ▽

The day Action drowns near Djifer the tide in Joal casts ashore a
man so decomposed that the only certain thing about him is that
he was a fisherman: the corpse is wearing a green slicker and
beige rubberized overalls. They bury him as soon as they find
him, right on the beach.

This often happens when men die at sea, say fishermen who
play cards in the eucalyptus shade between the hospital and the
weather advisory flagpole by Mbaar Sarrené. Been in the water
too long, too rotten to take to the cemetery. Such graves line the
coast, they say. There was one right there, under that flagpole,
see? I look: the flag flops yellow, warns of troubled seas.

But that grave is gone now.

Where we buried that man, the sea took it. Now he's in the
ocean.

Between here and the filao grove we probably buried ten
people.

More than that.

Maybe more than that.

I don't remember his name.

I don't think we ever knew his name.

Life is so.

Come on, it's your turn now.

The men resume their card game: belote, a game of tricks. The
wind smells of eucalyptus and raw fish. Bougainvillea branches
droop over the stucco walls of white people's vacation homes.

"The sea is never pregnant," a Wolof proverb goes: You can
never predict when it will deliver. You can never predict what it

will take, either. To live off the sea is to submit to its vagaries, to
endure constantly the tension between desire and defeat.

▽ ▲ ▽

I go looking for the grave of the man who washed up in the
morning. I walk toward the weather flag and then turn south
along the tideline.

Spring tide under a roiling sky, black black surf. I study the
shoreline. The shipwreck of it. A collage of windblown jacaranda
blossoms, fishnet tangles, turtle excrement, brown plastic cups,
fishheads, styrofoam floats studded with barnacles, fishhooks, and
birdbones caught in bales of maroon seaweed that is used to make
an additive that clarifies your beer and stabilizes your toothpaste.

Watch this elastic line erode. The onshore winds of the rainy
season—warm, humid, oily with salt—abrade the adobes of Joal,
winnow bricks out of their sockets. After a few years houses begin
to look cellular, like honeycombs. Pause by the wall of my rental
room: you can see minuscule white granules weather out in faint
diaphanous streams, sand seeping back into sand. You can hear
them. Or, much louder, in Palmarin, in Joal, in Saint-Louis, where
entire walls crash down onto the beach. Then the offshore winds
of the dry season come, push Africa into the ocean grain by grain.

I pass a pack of dogs gnawing a dead goat. There is something
terribly wrong with all the dogs here, the mangy, shorthaired yellow mutts that roam the town's tideline and sleep in pirogues'
shade. They are broken, ripped up, maggoty around the ears and

snouts. They skulk; when they lie in the road they barely raise their heads at passers-by. I am told they are mongrel descendants of the dogs the Portuguese slave traders brought along. A friend corrects me: the strays are probably laobé, an indigenous West African breed. Does it make any difference? The story is out; one way or another, the curs have become mnemonics for an unforgivable iniquity.

A skinny man follows me from the belote game. His name is Serigne Fallou, like the second Mouride caliph.

Serigne Fallou, are you a fisherman?

One hundred percent! By the way, the nearest grave is between here and that *mbaar*. I helped bury the man in that grave. But the sea took it.

At Mbaar Sarrené men mend net under a roof thatched with palm fronds. We *salaam* them, explain our quest. They respond by joking that a man who has only one wife will go to hell after death. Ha ha ha. And a man who dies a bachelor will burn in eternal fire. Ha ha ha! Many things on the shore seem non sequiturs to me.

Serigne Fallou continues his guided tour of the mariners' purgatory:

There was another one here. We didn't know him. We found him in the sea. I helped bury him, too. But the grave is no longer here. The sea took it.

The sand is crusty above the tideline, striated with scrapings of crabs. Under our footfalls it collapses, implodes. I think of drowning, its irrevocable and crushing loneliness.

How many fishermen have you helped bury?

Maybe ten.

Does that make it hard for you to go fishing?

Not really. I've seen so many dead fishermen by now, it doesn't really bother me.

Serigne Fallou did not see this morning's corpse. His neighbor found it. We telephone the neighbor, but he does not want to come to the shore to show us the spot. No, that would feel ghastly. It was ghastly in the morning already. The body was completely decomposed. It was lying facedown in the sand. All the hair was gone from its skull.

Serigne Fallou peels off. I go on looking. Suddenly before me is a geyser: thousands of creamy white butterflies are hatching out of a nopal grove. The butterflies are the banded goldtip, *Colotis eris eris*. They are native to Senegal. Nopal is an American transplant, another relic of the slave trade. I recall a poem, say the lines out loud: "So, in the undergrowth, they came together, / butterflies and the bones of the dead." It is okay to recite Neruda on the beach. On the tideline a few dozen yards away, a young athlete in a white singlet and blue gym shorts is singing, too, in English: "Wanna make up right now na na."

The fruit is ripe; I pick one, roll it in the sand with a broken cymbium shell to shuck the spines. On both sides of the ocean, prickly pear stains fingertips with juice that runs bloodred.

I eat, I watch the butterflies, I continue down the shore.

Then I see a grave in the filao grove, an elliptical shape topped with broken murex shells and trimmed with broken bricks. And then an unmarked bump in the sand cinched by dune creepers that reach their tendrils toward the ocean. And another, trussed to the shore by weathered brambles. And another unmarked rise, behind a young grove of Sodom's apples, whose leaves offer protection against the genii that snatch the souls of newborn babies. And this, a bleached boneyard of long conch shells and two cracked brown plastic coffee cups—who lies here? Another, and another. Are these burial mounds? Accidental sand drifts? It does not matter. The fishermen's grave is right here. Remorseless, greedy, eternally lapping against the shore.

"Great mother of life, the sea," wrote Rachel Carson. "The beginning and the end." I shudder: Somewhere in the sea there is the man's hair. And the hair and the bones of all the dead whose graves the sea has taken, whom it has taken to the grave. Things on Earth forever carry seaward. More than nine thousand cubic miles of water may flow into the sea each year, and with it billions of tons of salts, and millions of tons of plastic garbage, and bones mixed in the currents of riverwater and groundwater, migrating under our feet and paths and homes and kitchens. We are always walking on bones.

▽ ▲ ▽

Our ancestors buried one another aboard ships, or buried ships alongside. More than four thousand years ago someone sealed into the ground at the foot of the Great Pyramid of Giza a carvel-planked solar barge one hundred and forty-three feet long: a funereal vessel that was never meant to sail in this world. We know it as the Khufu ship. Anglo-Saxons in the sixth and seventh centuries buried noblemen inside boats that appear seaworthy. Ahmad ibn Fadhlân, a tenth-century traveling merchant from Baghdad, wrote of a Viking cremation aboard the boat of a wealthy dead man in Russia. Also in the flames aboard this ark: his horses, cows, chickens, weapons, food, and a slave woman; before setting her on fire the mourners gang-raped, stabbed, and strangled her. They marked the site of the pyre with a birch post on which they wrote the man's name, not the woman's. For two millennia between the Nordic Bronze Age and the Viking Age, a thousand years before the Common Era and a thousand after, Scandinavians arranged stone slabs around some burial sites in the lanceolate shape of boats. Archaeologists call those stone ships.

In Saint-Louis—the first capital of French West Africa, the colonial slaving center, the Venice of Senegal—a narrow cemetery stretches nearly a mile in the dunes of the western peninsula of Langue de Barbarie between fish smokers' tarnished stands and the asphalt road of the harbor. One grave is bordered by pirogue planks, blues and reds and yellows yet unfaded. Maybe the pirogue's owner is interred here. Or maybe this, too, was a wash-up, the ocean's gruesome gift. The grave bears no name.

I hold to my ear the shell I used to clean the prickly pear. I imagine I will hear some old maritime memories that have swirled into its spiral, curlicued there. But the conch only amplifies the immeasurable sound of emptiness: the indifferent sea that has shaped its curves, that has shaped our continents' curves, that shapes our short unremembered lives and unmemorable deaths.

▽ ▲ ▽

After lunch I visit my neighbor, Mamour's second wife, Yacine. She is twenty-eight, a mother of four. Her body is long, flowing. She moves as if she is not serious about moving, as if every step is a joke, a tease she tosses at you. When she smiles it is as if she knows a secret for which you are too young.

Yacine greets me with that smile. Her hair is straightened, with a blond highlight. Her mermaid skirt is a pattern of large pink shrimp on a green field. She takes me by the hand and walks me through her submarine blue hallway and offers me a plastic chair to sit in. She takes one for herself. She leaves the front door open. Mamour is not home from fishing yet. She moves my chair so that I, too, can watch the door.

While we drink sweet tea with mint the western sea in the doorframe turns green then purple then the palest yellowish blue, then black. Mamour is very late today. Have you called him? Ha, he doesn't have a phone. She has called the harbor, where boats unload their catch of the day. They said the *Mansor Sakho* has not yet arrived. Actually, let me call again. No, not there yet.

Finally it is so dark the sea is just a vastness beyond the compound walls, a thick indigo void. Yacine straps her nine-month-old girl, her youngest, to her back and moves her chair. In its place, at the farthest end of the hallway, under the portraits of the

Mouride caliphs, she lays a plastic mat and covers it with a polyester blanket. She shucks off her sandals, steps onto the blanket, and begins to dance.

Step step. Step step. It is for the baby, she explains. To quiet her down. But the girl, who is often whiny, has not made a sound this evening, not even a pout. Yacine dances facing the sea. Long-limbed, slow-bodied, like a queen. Step step. Step step. She looks at the door.

My god, I think, she watches that door every day.

It is past dinnertime when a teenage boy walks in, one of her husband's crew. He took a taxi from the harbor. Thirteen boxes of sardine today, he reports, a good day. The pirogue is on her way home. Yacine just keeps on dancing. Step step. Step step. She does not change pace, does not take her eyes off the door.

I have begun, on evening walks, to scan the moorings for familiar boats.

▽ ▲ ▽

A waitress in a small fishing village upcoast takes my order—grilled shrimp, she recommends, delicious—then tells me her husband died at sea. What do you do with such knowledge? Lying there on the table before you: the salt and pepper shakers, the place mat, the plate of peanuts, and this. Idiotically, self-servingly you try to undo it, force it impossible: she's much too young to have had a husband! No no, madame, she laughs, gracious, firm, rejecting your insensitive offer to erase her loss.

No, it is true, I have two children, one is already in first grade, I'll go tell the kitchen to get started on your order now—and you are left to fold and refold this new story of heartbreak like a napkin.

▽ ▲ ▽

That day a purse seiner clips the *Sakhari Souaré* at sea. An accident, nothing major. She is in dry dock between Mbaar Kanené and Mbaar Atelier Taïf with a large gash in her port bow. In her chain locker a ramhorn gris-gris dangles on a length of red twine. Did it protect her from foundering altogether? Did it do anything at all? Ndongo finds a loaner, a twenty-six-foot pirogue. But when the crew arrive at the tideline the following morning before the sun they cannot spot her at first. Then they see in the surf the gleam of her gunwales. She is awash.

For the next few days the Souarés have three broken pirogues on their hands, and none to fish in.

▽ ▲ ▽

The thin mocking smile of a crescent moon rises pink over the thieving sea. A new month begins, Diggi-gàmmu, the second month of the Wolof calendar. Its Arabic name is Safar: hollow, zero, the whistling of the wind. A month of misfortune and calamities, when men leave home.

They hold a memorial service for Action on the fourth morning of the month. A bodiless funeral in a sandy alley just north of the hospital and Mbaar Sarrené and its pointless flag. I know this alley: I run through it every dawn when I am not at sea. I recognize its drooping bougainvillea and the red iron shutters of the Fouta Torro Shop, which did not close for the funeral, and from which now young boys push past the mourners clutching their breakfast *pain au chocolat* baguettes.

The funeral tent is a green and orange tarp. Under it on mats and plastic chairs three dozen or so old men are whispering Koranic verses in unison. The rest of the mourners, about two hundred in all, sit outside in facing rows that run along the crumbling yellow and pink stucco of the alley's houses. They sit on narrow seablue benches borrowed from one of the parochial elementaries, in metal chairs upholstered in a faded red, on wooden benches fashioned from discarded pirogue planks: pirogues furnish forth all, even funeral pews. They sit in blue and white molded plastic chairs—the same enumerated chairs in which men sat in the harbor during the sacrifice several days before. The community chairs of Joal, some of them my landlord's, make the rounds of funerals, sacrifices, naming ceremonies, weddings.

Mostly young men in the chairs this time—Action's friends, in their flipflops and suave footballer hairdos and secondhand tee shirts with sequins and famous logos and denim jeans or gym pants that ride under their buttocks, show off their boxer shorts. They spread their knees, rest their elbows, clasp their hands, lower their heads, mouth prayers. A young man in a Juventus tee shirt cradles a toddler. I recognize a fisherman with whom I have fished aboard the *Mansor Sakho*. His name is Ibrahima but they call him Gambia because he is from there. He is twenty-two, his Wolof and English softly stuttered. He has been crying. He prays into his upturned palms, then sits back, leans against the wall, blinks.

More men arrive. Older men in long boubous, young men in denim and track suits. We scoot over to make room. Sit tighter together. Feel one another's breath, heartbeat, sweat, life. Matronly women in lace file through the alley, head inside Action's family compound, on the other side of the tent, where they will mourn away from the men.

Older men talk.

Fishermen here don't respect the idea of wearing life jackets. But a life jacket would have been very useful.

Yes, even if he'd drowned at least they would have found his body.

Strong currents down in Djifer. They can carry you away and there's nothing you can do.

The current there probably took him to the mangroves.

If it took him to the mangroves then his body will get tangled in the roots. It will slowly rot, they'll never find him.

Did they call the gendarmes?

What can the gendarmes do? They are on land; the boy is in the water.

Well, we are praying for him anyway.

He had a bad back. He had some metal rods in his back even, maybe that's why he drowned.

At least they got the pirogue.

What's the name of the pirogue?

Oh, I don't know it.

Oh, she has no name.

But she does of course. The *Fatou Ndiaye*, named after the grandmother of my landlord, who was a sorceress. She belongs to a fisherman named Pape Yakha, who is out of town today, but the day Action drowned the captain was Pape Sow. There he is, sitting a bit to the side, far from the tent, in a blue boubou. He looks both young and old.

So what? It could have been any pirogue here.

Amen.

⋎ ⋏ ⋎

A breeze.

The men have finished murmuring suras from the Koran and it is very quiet. Women come out of the compound, hand out plastic baggies of animal crackers and *naq*, balls of steamed millet flour spiced with cloves, a snack traditional for ceremonies. We stash the repast between our knees, cup our hands, prepare for the prayer for the dead.

The old Pa Souleimane Sarr speaks:

Salaam aleikum. I am speaking because the family's elders asked me to speak to you. I thank you for coming and may God accept our prayers and accept Mansour's soul in paradise. The Prophet said we must praise the dead. Mansour was educated, polite, respectful, and hardworking. He didn't have good health, but he never asked others to work for him. God is able to help all the people in the world. May God help him and give him mercy.

Amen.

God gave Mansour to us and He took him again. May God help us so we can live without another such tragedy at sea again for many years.

Amen.

I look at Gambia, at all the other boys across the alley. Sassy, muscled, handsome, young. Eventually their friend's remains will wash up on some shore where boys like them will bury him in an unmarked grave in the sand. Aren't all graves unmarked? Can a name, a date, mark the absence and sorrow the dead leave in their wake?

The sun balls its heat in my palms.

▽ ▵ ▽

A friend, a sometime tour guide in Joal, tells me about a woman he knows whose son died fishing:

She said—I know it's funny—"I will never eat fish again."

Why is it funny, El Hadji?

I don't know. Life continues. If you don't eat fish, what do you eat?

Action's mother is Marie Badiane. Her husband, Action's father, lives with his second wife in some other town and sometimes sends money back to Joal, but not regularly. This is common; life is so. Marie is a fishwife at the port—one of those women who wade up to their armpits in harbor swill to bargain with fishermen back from the sea. Everywoman. On the day of the funeral, after dark, I stand in her doorway.

Marie is dressed in burgundy. Her cinderblock house, a single rectangular room, is burgundy and purple inside. Faux silk and velvet curtains and bedspread. Severe furniture. An incense stick smolders on the floor; smoke curls in dim mirrors. The only light comes from a flashlight that stands upright on one of the dressers. Next to it an expensive-looking shiny sound system gleams, Action's.

She sits on the edge of that purple bed and talks fast:

I remember you! You were on that purse seiner with your notebook writing something and I called out to you, "How are you?" and you said, "I am well!" Remember? I thought it was funny to see a woman on a pirogue. And now you're here, in my house! Thank you for coming. Thank you, thank you—here, let me show you his photo. Where is his photo? Eh! Where is his photo?

Women swarm into this cube of grief, look for the photo, it was just here—are you sitting on it?—no, it is in someone else's room—here it is. Here. Look! This is my boy. A laminated enlarged printout of him standing with his girlfriend, who now will be raising alone their six-month-old child. She is statuesque in beige brocade. He is in a black tee shirt emblazoned with a gangster logo in silver gothic letters, copper protection bangles, a Chicago Bulls cap, red Converse lace-ups. Swag. Out of the scented purple dark Marie smiles at me. He's handsome, isn't he.

I return to my room to make a call to Ohio, to my own son,

who is two years younger than Action and very far from the sea.
A day's allocation of sand has seeped out of the wall onto my
sleeping mat and upon it waits a pale butterfly.

▽ △ ▽

The next day a flotilla of two sails out of Joal: a purse seiner
crewed mostly by strong young men who cast and haul the
heavy net, and her catch boat: a typically lightly manned receptacle
to carry the fish to harbor. The catch boat's crew are Bathie
Diakayaté, a twenty-three-year-old orphan who has never gone to
sea before, and his cousin Oumar Kane, the tenth and youngest
son of a fisherman. Oumar is twelve. The pirogue, the *Khady
Sarr*—forty-two feet, forty-horsepower motor—bears his mother's
name.

The tandem hauls anchor early, aiming to be back by dinnertime. Fifteen miles offshore, in international waters, the catch
boat's motor malfunctions. The net boat's captain tells the cousins
to drop anchor and wait for his return while he catches some sardines. A few hours, max. He takes their coordinates. The sustained wind of the dry season shatters the Atlantic into spangled
eddies of black jewels. The *Khady Sarr* bobs on the sparkling sea,
rocks the cousins to sleep.

But the captain's GPS records incorrectly the *Khady Sarr*'s coordinates. When the net boat returns for the boys in the afternoon, they are not there.

The cold wakes the child. It is night now, the wind blows raw. Bathie, too, shivers awake. In the dark the ocean bleeds black into endless black sky. The boys see a pirogue's green prow light, hear an approaching motor. They have a flashlight; they blink it at the light, beckoning. The pirogue passes, the sound of her motor dies, and now it is only the two of them atop the vast and terrible womb of everything.

The pirogues' owner, Coura Kane, a distant relative of Oumar, organizes a search party, but it is brief, because he is too poor to foot the fuel bill, and unsuccessful. Khady Sarr, Oumar's mother, crazed by fear, grovels on the tideline, trying to stare her son and nephew out of the horizon. I run into Coura at Mbaar Kanené, the one he helped build, on the morning of the third day, his eyes bloodshot from vigil and weeping, a sheaf of papers in his hands. He and Daouda Sarr and Malal Diallo have been petitioning one government office in town after another to organize a proper search. Bureaucrats keep asking for more papers. The fishermen sit in a kind of stupor, worry the prayer beads of their grievances and sorrows.

The coastguard comes here to do surveillance for traffickers or if there are drugs—but they will not lift their finger for lost fishermen, *wallahi*.

They are just eating our money.

In Senegal the government only tells fishermen to pay. It's not helping us at all.

They tax our boats and give our fisheries to foreign trawlers and they tell us we can't fish near the shore. If this continues there will not be any fishing left in Joal.

If there isn't fish again next year there won't be any money.

If we're even here next year.

A couple years ago we tried to put a GPS chip in the boat but it didn't work.

After Ramadan there was a boat with seven men and a new motor that went for a weeklong trip. We never saw them again.

That's why I never go on long trips, says Coura. Once I was very far from shore, we were fifty fathoms deep. This was off Freetown. And suddenly there was something in the water, man. Someone said it was a ship, and someone said an island, and we sailed toward it and it just disappeared.

He is staring into nothing now, far away, young and scared shitless again on that long-ago pirogue.

Man, once you survive such a thing you never want to do it again. It was gone. When we sailed up to it, it was gone. I was so scared I said, we're turning back, man, to keep going is suicide.

I'll only go on a long trip for octopus. It's not far and it's not that long.

When you fish shark you can go days without seeing another boat. I'm a fisherman, but I know the sea is very dangerous. Once a friend was taking a pirogue to Spain and he offered me four spots. I said, No, thank you. It's true that it's up to God to decide when we die but we should take care of ourselves, too.

▽ ⩒ ▽

A t the harbor a clerk at the regional branch of the ministry of fishing sends Coura away three times to fetch documents and copies of documents. On Coura's fourth visit he approves the paperwork but refuses to telephone the coastguard in Dakar for help finding the lost boys. Surveillance is very expensive. Besides, in Senegal children shouldn't work, so Oumar Kane is breaking the law. Anyway, the cousins went fishing at night before the night-fishing season opens so they must be simply looking for a place to move their illegal catch. To my insistence he responds: You are a woman and a mother, of course you think with your heart.

At last the officer who handles surveillance for the marine refuge receives Coura and Malal in his corner office. There is air-conditioning. There is a massive desk with a large swivel chair, an army cot in the corner, dog-eared marine charts tacked to a drafting table, a life jacket resting on a dresser. We sit in metal chairs before the desk, watch the officer thumb through the papers Coura has brought. The title for the net boat and the catch boat. Registration for both. Tax forms. A copy of Coura's identity card. The officer lays them out on the desk. Shuffles them again into a pile. Leans back, studies us. Coura and Malal sit with their hands in their laps, skinny, ashy, small.

The officer links his fingers at his navel.

So. No life jackets on board. You have to wear life jackets. You have to make an effort! A cheap life jacket isn't that expensive. You fishermen, you only care about having some money and something to eat. But you must prepare. When you go to sea and you have twenty crew, you need to bring food for thirty. If you are going for a day, bring water for three days. If you think you'll need three hundred liters of gas, bring four hundred.

We can't afford that, says Coura.

Pah! A small problem onboard can cost your lives. Look here. See this? You know what this is? A mirror, made in America. You fishermen will say, we are not women, we don't need mirrors. But!

He raises an admonishing forefinger.

It's not for your vanity. It's for your safety! You use it as a reflector, to draw attention to the boat. You put it on a string—like this, see?—and you put the string around your neck so that you always have it with you. And on the other end of the same string there is a whistle. Like this.

He puts the whistle to his mouth, pretends to blow. A grounded flight attendant performing a safety demonstration.

Now. See this? This is a dye. If your anchor line snaps and you are afloat you put this in the water so that people can track your movement. See this? A flare—

Coura sinks into his chair. Malal stares away. The lecture curls inward upon itself like a shoaling wave.

And you must memorize the pirogue's license number because everyone's boat is named after the same damned caliph. Do you know how many *Khady Sarr*s are there in Senegal? Even here in Joal—

Coura has had it. He leaps up, stomps over to the dresser, jabs his right forefinger into the orange life vest.

Give me this life jacket.

No.

Give it to me.

No, it's mine!

Give it!

No! Okay, I will call the coastguard for you now.

He digs for his cellphone, dials a number. Dictates the *Khady Sarr*'s registration number and length, the make of her motor, the names of the missing crew. The coastguard won't go looking for the pirogue but it will radio all the ships in the vicinity that have a radio onboard. Maybe this will help. Outside his window tall filao trees conceal the only lighthouse in Joal, a squat tower of rebar and concrete, obscure the sea view of the flashing beacon. Behind the lighthouse and the trees the ocean turns green then ocher then gray then black. Somewhere on it is the lost pirogue.

∇ ▲ ∇

That evening, gillnet captain Paul Maurice Diouf accidentally runs across the *Khady Sarr* on his way to port. Three days and two nights after they were abandoned at sea, the boys, scared, hungry, alive, are towed to shore. A few weeks after their rescue, the cousins will be fishing again. What else is there? Their crewmates continue to sail, their boats continue to haul net, empty or full.

▽ ▲ ▽

Steady northeast wind. Harmattan cloaks the shore. An ophthalmologist at the town hospital painfully turns my right eyelid inside out to shake out beach sand that has lodged there. At sea before sunup the moon is a cold fish in the sky. The ocean is bluegreen and choppy and the *Mansor Sakho* vibrates as she heads southwest. She did not fish yesterday and when the crew shake out her net, dust and fish scales fly. The sea turns emerald, then turquoise.

The day at sea is jerky, stop and go, shellacked in wind-water.

Eleven-fifteen. The *Mansor Sakho* is at anchor twenty nautical miles offshore, in high seas: *mare liberum*, free sea. She has been lying safe for over an hour. The stiff wind keeps the fish at the bottom; to look for schools in this weather is to waste fuel. Around us, other anchored boats on a surface brilliantly rippled. All the pirogues still like trout, waiting. Wind carries the chatter of fishermen, the reggae on someone's cellphone.

The wind's dying down.

Yes, it always does this time of day.

When it stops we'll see fish.

Hôpital is asleep facedown on the net as usual, arms raised above his head. On his left wrist a golden Dolce & Gabbana watch with a cracked crystal, its bezel trimmed with rhinestones that flash at the sea. The sea flashes back. The watch does not work. As far as Hôpital knows it never did. He picked it up at the house where he is renting a room and wears it because it makes his wrist look pretty.

Eh, Hôpital!

He stirs awake.

What's the time?

He sleeps again. Facedown, arms raised, knees akimbo: I draw him in my sketchbook. The crew demand to see the sketch, pass it around, take photographs of it with their cellphones. That's him, that's our Hôpital, that big head, always sleeping! They kick Hôpital to wake him, show him the picture. He is upset.

Did you see me sleep? I never sleep!

He begins to roll a joint, then changes his mind, puts the vial with dope back into the plastic bag he stashes under a thwart, lies down again, closes his eyes.

Hôpital trained as a carpenter but switched to fishing twenty-three years ago. He was about twenty then. He likes fishing better. Life is simpler. You smoke and work and eat and sleep and smoke and sleep again. You rock in the crib of the net hold.

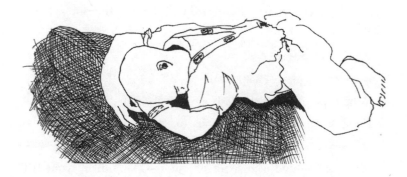

▽ ▲ ▽

At quarter to noon the pirogue sails again. Twenty-five miles off the coast of Sangomar a cricket starts in the stern, starts and stops, starts and stops. A stowaway. Cricket season began after the two funerals; the insects slam into my tiled floor at night and in the morning ants disassemble them and carry their parts toward the manger in dutiful funerary processions. Their bustle makes my tiny room feel crowded.

A small pirogue sails by, a trapsetter with a lone man aboard. He points: Fish that way.

Aboard the *Mansor Sakho*, arms wide apart: A school?

The man nods, points again: Yes, that way.

Mamour steers that way.

At two-thirty the men cast and the unfurling net, unused for a day, releases a stench of ammonia and fish oil and a swarm of blowflies and a butterfly or two. Black blowfly larvae fall to the bottom of the boat. The net sinks; an orange praying mantis bobs up, struggles on slender legs toward the boat in a fine slick of boat fuel.

Work, men, work!

Thank you, men! Thank you!

When you get paid the cash is yours to use!

If you keep it up we'll be done quickly!

Work-work-work-work-work!

Men pass around a jerrycan of water—Don't drink your fill!

Have a sip then pass it on or we'll run out!—then one, two, three men jump overboard and Mamour grabs the hammer and begins to whack the port gunwhale. Men knock with burden boards, the cinchrope rings clang, the motor smokes and rumbles. Under the black sea the trapped fish begin to glint. It takes fifteen minutes for all of them to pour into the hold. More than a ton of sardines. They slap, slap, calm. Men rinse off, roll joints, smoke, eat, smoke again. I bail. I have been sitting downwind of their pot smoke for so long that I am stoned.

▿ ▲ ▿

Quarter to five, twelve nautical miles offshore, territorial waters boundary unmarked. The pirogue rocks lightly on following seas. Suddenly a swarm of creamy butterflies pours over her, fore to aft. A milky runnel of banded goldtips streams away from shore southward except for one, which turns at the stern and continues back toward Joal alongside the pirogue—a winged escort, an airborne protector genie, now sitting down on a gunwale, now lifting off again until it, too, breaks off and vanishes in the blue afternoon.

At half past five the sun is less than a palm above western sea, the harbor close, the fishermen quiet. Pa Pape Ndiaye stands up on a thwart to pray. He stands over the fish in the bilges, over the turquoise hull and the darkening ocean that buoys it. A shirtless old man, small and creased and very black in oversize rubber trousers and kneehigh rubber boots. He raises his palms to his ears, mouths his devotion, bows. Bows again. Then he lifts his hands to his face, palms downward, and whispers something onto his knuckles and in the grooves between them, and then blows his whispers away, down the thin misshapen fingers that have hauled net almost daily for almost fifty years, and blows them all the way into the sea. The gesture is so vulnerable and his face so delicately soft he is unbearable to watch.

Six

Nearly four billion years ago, the first life-forms appeared in Earth's young seas. They could process inorganic materials into glucose, turn non-life into life; scientists call such magic biopoiesis. Their molecules had accumulated enough chemical knowledge to make decisions based on their environment, which means life and free will originated in synchrony, possibly in gassy plumes of hydrothermal vents that conveyed heat from the planet's molten innards to the water's surface. "Barely over the intangible line that separates the non-living from the living," Rachel Carson wrote of these initial organisms. Borderline beings, each an ecotone of its own.

Eons removed from those transitional creatures, we, too, contain our own borderlands, which we endlessly discover, establish, revise. A lifelong task: we shift them to accommodate a lover, guard them when they keep us whole, blot them out to remain

open to wonderment. Such continuous imperma-
nence informs our humanness; to probe it is intro-
spection sublime. Maybe this is why I come aboard
pirogues that belong both to our future and our
past, ancient vessels that sail on the latest twostroke
engines; why I help build one.

▽ ▲ ▽

That weekend Joal falls quiet. Shorthanded boats rest at anchor.
Half the town has left on an annual pilgrimage that commemorates the first arrest and exile of the founder of the Mouride Sufi
brotherhood, Cheikh Amadou Bamba Mbacké, and takes his dev-
otees to the holy city of Touba. The pilgrimage is called Magal
Touba.

Magal: to celebrate, to praise, to grace. Magal Touba takes
place on the eighteenth day of Diggi-gàmmu, which this year
falls on the first of December, the opening day of the night-
fishing season. The Mourides consider the journey equal to the
hajj. Millions of people come. Sufis from other orders—the Tijaan,
the Qadri, the Layenne—join the rite because all agree that
Bamba was a visionary.

Cheikh Amadou Bamba—Ahmad bin Muhammad bin Habib
Allah, Servant of the Messenger, Caliph of Touba—was a son of a
Toucouleur marabout and an indirect descendant of the Prophet
Muhammad. He was an ascetic pacifist preacher; French colonists
imprisoned and exiled him twice on the charges of fomenting
rebellion, then knighted him as a Legionnaire of Honor. In 1887,

Bamba designed and created from scratch in the barren scrub-
lands of the Sahel the city of Touba as the model of a perfect Islamic society, a Muslim utopia where all sin was forbidden and
where rigorous earthly labor coexisted with religious scholarship.
Indeed, in Bamba's vision, hard work represents spiritual devotion. He authored twenty thousand mystical verses in Arabic on
pacifism, hard work, and good manners. It is said he was the
original maker of café Touba.

Only one photograph of Bamba exists. It is overexposed, his
shadow is short: a midmorning or midafternoon. He stands facing
the camera in leather sandals and a white boubou that ends at the
shin. The sleeves cover his hands entirely. Underfoot, beach sand;
behind him, a shingled wooden wall and a simple wooden door.
A white headscarf obscures most of his face, but you can see his
wrinkled forehead and narrowed eyes: he is squinting against the
sun. Despite the scarf his face seems open, candid. Maybe it is his
posture. Bamba wrote: "I performed my repentance to Allah. He
forgave me for everything and veiled my imperfection by the
Elected One."

▼ ▲ ▼

Christian faith centers on the fear of the everlasting punishment of hell. "I can fancy the tortures of the damned,"
Flannery O'Connor wrote in her journal, "but I cannot imagine
the disembodied souls hanging in a crystal for all eternity praising
God." But in Islam, heaven is specific, with gardens of perpetual

bliss and plentiful feasts and infinite scented valleys, an eternity spent conversing with rejuvenated loved ones by misty waterfalls. When I point out the difference to a Senegalese writer, my friend laughs: Hell is already here, he says. We are in it.

In a world filled with suffering, suffering has little value, wretchedness repels. Hagiography of Bamba's life chooses his miracles over his martyrdom.

When his French captors locked him up in a cage with a hungry lion Bamba prayed the beast to sleep. When they threw him in a furnace he used the fire to make tea and the Prophet joined him for a cup. When they sent a mad bull to charge him in a narrow street in Dakar the bull jumped over him "as if it had wings:" Lamassu, the Assyrian protector deity, momentarily summoned.

Bamba's most fabled miracle took place at sea. This makes sense. The ocean's salt vapor diffracts, magnifies everything— even magic.

Shackled aboard the ship deporting him from Saint-Louis to his seven-year exile in the rainforest of Gabon in 1895, Bamba was forbidden to pray. But not praying would have meant offending God, and this contradicted Bamba's own teachings: he preached religious submission and respect. So he broke free of his manacles, tossed his prayer mat into the ocean, jumped overboard, alighted on the floating rug, and made his devotions. Then he folded the rug and, carrying it under one arm, walked upon the waves back to his prison ship. To honor this miracle, at one point during the daylong sacrament of Magal Touba the pilgrims in the city's streets turn their backs on Mecca and pray seaward. Just one prayer out of the day's five. Just one prayer out of a life's multitudes.

Many of the pilgrims are fishermen. They rely on miracles for a living. They know that a good catch, like heaven, is specific and attainable if you follow the guidelines. The guidelines are the same for both—sacrifice, prayer, wise marabouts, strong gris-gris—though God has the last word in either case. Neither abides by laws of science because faith requires no proof.

But look. The proof is written: a promise of plenty, by Bamba himself. "Make my right hand and my heart provide generosity and abundance," he wrote, "like the ocean." And so they hush, and pray directly at the Atlantic, whose waters carry their fortunes and their sorrows and their dead.

Bamba died in 1927 under house arrest in the town of Diourbel, between Dakar and Touba. He is buried in Touba, inside the rose marble of the Grande Mosquée, which he had designed. "My writings," he wrote, "are my true miracles."

▽ ▲ ▽

After Magal the pilgrims hurry back to their chores, families, the sea. There is a stampede. Thirteen people die and four hundred and sixty-six are injured in nearly one hundred traffic accidents on the way out of Bamba's holy city.

▽ ▲ ▽

Just before dawn a wispy pink flag of cloud lights up vermilion in the southeast. Through its fraying edge, from a sky lavender and blue, Venus winks at another star, in the water: a bowlight. Between these two beacons my neighbor, a fisherman named Mico Sene, is preparing to send out his beached abachi trapsetter with a crew of three to hunt for cuttlefish. It is small-crafts-warning weather; morning reports forecast a gale. The trapsetter will sail twelve miles offshore.

The pirogue is named the *Sope Naby*: the Prophet's Disciples. She is thirty feet long, with a beam of less than three feet. Her slender hull is painted port and starboard with American flags shaped like hearts that are flanked by the ensigns of Senegal and France. Mico's three favorite countries. Why? I just like them, they are good countries. It's for beauty, like the flowers on your dress. Up and down the coast boat hulls and the caving façades of houses are painted with foreign flags. American. Spanish. Italian. German. French. Flags of desire, crumbling to the sea.

Mico checks the jigging lines, the hooks, the harpoons. He has heard the forecast so he brings five orange life jackets to the shore and throws them in the forward hold bilge. Then he piles on top of them the fourteen heavy traps made of rebar and wide-caliber net that he has baited with dead skates, fills the traps with filao branches. Cuttlefish will enter the traps for a bite of skate flesh, or to attach to the brushy filao the ink-dyed capsules of eggs that

Aristotle likened to bunches of grapes. Cuttlefish mate for death: The males will die after mating, though some will live long enough to guard the female until she lays her clutch. The females will die after the eggs hatch. The Senegalese have no taste for cuttlefish, which they consider inferior to most other seafood, so this mollusk is for export only, which means that at the harbor cuttlefish pays much better than sardines do. The buoyant ellipsoid cuttlebones will become jewelers' casting molds or ground calcium supplements for pet reptiles and caged birds. The flesh will become an entrée, an appetizer, a beer snack. The thick dark ink will dye pastas and rice: it is from the mollusk genus, *Sepia*, that the brown pigment and the coloration of early monochrome photographs derive their shared name. Juveniles and the smaller

African cuttlefish, *S. bertheloti*, fetch more per pound because their flesh is more tender, but large fifteen-pounders, *S. hierredda* or *S. officinalis*, fill the holds quicker.

The crew arrive: Moussa Sene, twenty-four and saving up for a farm inland; Elhadj Dieye, twenty-two and saving up for computer mechanic college in Dakar; and the captain, Djiby Diop, who is nineteen years old and is not saving up for anything: he is just fishing. Djiby has been fishing since he was seven. He is the only married man on the crew and his wife is very pregnant with their second child. Their first, a boy, was stillborn.

It is dark when we push the *Sope Naby* into frigid winter whitecaps, but by the time the crew have prayed, the sun, not yet visible, flushes the foaming sea a hammered lustrous yellow. Along the ocean's thin black rim purse seiners return to harbor from a night of fishing. In the bow Elhadj boils water on a brazier, mixes powdered milk with sugar for his crewmates. The morning is cold enough for windbreakers, for sweaters under the rubberized overalls and slickers. Djiby and Elhadj pull their wool skullcaps down low. Djiby shivers against the wind, washes down his pain au chocolat breakfast with sweet hot milk, steers northward.

By eight o'clock the fresh gale turns severe. The waves are nine feet tall. Ten. Twelve. Striped green and blue and white seas throw the *Sope Naby* this way and that. The little boat lurches about, now awash in the high chop of the following seas, now groaning up and over nearly vertical head billows. She pounds. She nearly turtles as she heaves. Her fifteen-horsepower outboard floods, recovers. Djiby uses the motor to drogue her carefully but she plunges nonetheless. We are soaked in spindrift, in bilgewater, in ocean water. The shore is gone behind the horizon and the horizon is gone behind the heaped-up sea and the sun is gone in blowing foam. You know it is still there only by the rainbows that come and go, come and go, puff by on crests shredded over and over to spray.

Once upon a time mollusk grounds were like sardine fisheries: first come, first served. Now so many jiggers and trappers and dredgers flag to the Petite Côte that mollusk fishermen divvy up the sea, mark their territory with buoy flags they construct out of plastic, fabric, bamboo sticks, styrofoam floats, cans. On your way to the fishing grounds you pass through forests of flags. You can tell by their spacing if they attach to murex or cymbium nets, shadefish trammels, octopus or cuttlefish traps. If you have been fishing in the same waters long enough you can tell their ownership by their coloration. Mico's murex flags are red and black, cut from plastic tarp, and his cuttlefish flags are dirty white styrofoam orbs overgrown with seaweed and barnacle, spaced a hundred feet or so apart. In calm waters you see a flag field approach from a mile away or more. In a gale you are upon it suddenly and piecemeal: individual flags thrust up out of waves, appear on crests like desperate hands reaching from below. Their unseen lines snag your outboard.

A little after nine in the morning Djiby yells over the storm and the motor:

Should be here somewhere!

Where's your GPS?

Eh, I left it at home!

I think a little thataway!

Yeah, I think you're right!

Head seas, beam seas, overhanging waves topple. Madness to be out in this. Impossibly, Elhadj and Moussa stand up amidships. Elhadj wields an eight-foot bamboo harpoon with a metal hook the length of an index finger, Moussa a jigger in an outthrust hand. Funambulists, holding on to this tackle for balance in quartering waves. Performing for no audience but the tumbling sea.

Djiby stands up jackknifed in the stern and yells again.

Shit! Look at this storm! You see what the sea is like nowadays! This is bullshit! I need to do something else! Maybe I should take up farming!

Ah ha ha! You, Djiby—you will grow old on the sea!

Djiby, you will die a fisherman!

Okay, focus, boys, focus! These winds will die by noon! We got work to do!

The boat bounces and slams against the waves. For the next three hours the *Sope Naby* crawls over surges and plunges into troughs from one buoy to the next. The men seem to find them by instinct. Elhadj harpoons traps out of the water. Some empty. Some full of sea urchins, of cymbium snails seeping out of their plaited whorled shells. Some traps rattled apart by months of waves and tides. Some still neatly wrapped in their inch-wide netting. In this gale it takes twenty minutes to locate and haul and check one trap. There are cuttlefish in two out of the first ten.

Each time Elhadj harpoons a trap, Djiby idles the pirogue and he and Moussa wrap jigger line around their index fingers, dangle orange and blue sinkers corollaed with hooks like daisies of death. Moussa jerks at the line with his entire forearm; Djiby moves only his forefinger in tiny circular motions, as if caressing between a woman's legs. Two times out of three Djiby catches a cuttlefish, tosses it in the center hold. Moussa catches nothing at all.

Eh, Farmboy! says Djiby.

It's because of the waves! says Moussa.

Look, the traps are empty, too! In stormy seas the cuttlefish lay low, says Elhadj.

Yeah, but for Farmboy here all days are created equally fishless! says Djiby.

The three men laugh.

Farmboy is such a good gardener, Elhadj says to appease his crewmate, that he works at the villas owned by French people and can prune Arabic calligraphy into a shrubbery.

Farmboy is such a good laamb wrestler, says Djiby, that once he even won four Zebu cows, though one of them died. Besides, Farmboy gets all the girls! *Wallahi*, I swear one day I'll cut off his dick and hide it so he can never find it again.

The men laugh some more. Djiby lets the pirogue heave, steadies her.

Seriously though, when I started fishing, as a kid, I'd go with my dad, there was much more fish. And so much cuttlefish! I know I've been giving Farmboy shit about his jiggering, but the problem is that, really, none of us is catching anything today.

What are they doing out here, then, in these heaped waves? And what I am doing on their tumbledown pirogue? On any pirogue at all?

Psst, Anna, look!

Djiby interrupts my wallowing. He has harpooned a four-pounder with a bamboo pole and now flicks it to midships. The thing rotates into the hold like a tentacled frisbee and, in flight, jets an inksac full of mucus-bound melanin: a sprinkler from Hades, a marine Jackson Pollock. My right ear and my mouth are full of cold, salty viscousness. A christening, I think, a blessing with hallowed ink.

I smile—and notice then that my fingers have been gripping the gunwales so tightly for so long and in such bitter seas that I cannot unbend them to wipe my face. Stuck this way, I start to giggle, and ink dribbles out of my mouth and down my chin and now I cannot stop laughing: What poetic justice, what poetry indeed that the oceanborn free will in my chromosomal memory has guided me through wars and deserts and back to the sea to surrender so absolutely that I cannot even clean my face of cuttlefish ink.

▽ △ ▽

One day an *oupa* on a gillnetter hands me a cuttlefish no larger than a plum. We are bailing together; he finds the cuttlefish in the bilgewater. The little mollusk squirts ink, crawls down my palm, leaking black. When it runs out of water to

replenish the inksac it begins to suckle. Or so it seems at first—
a familiar strangeness, that dependent burrowing roundness of
a mouth. Then it bites. A perfect oval cuttlefish bitemark, nine
teeth, remains on my right index finger for months.

▽ ▵ ▽

By one in the afternoon at last the wind calms, the waves
flatten, stretch out into a splendid gilded snakeskin. The sun
burns at once. In the bow crickets sing in the traps, in the crushed
and forgotten life jackets. In the distance a seagull sits on the
water, pecking at something afloat. Djiby steers toward it: a large
cuttlefish, dead. At the pirogue's approach the seagull flies off,
drips white shit into cat's-paw seas. Djiby lifts the cuttlefish out
of the water, inspects it. A seven-pounder. He tosses it into the
bilge. Cuttlefish hauled dead sell at the harbor as long as they are
not disfigured too badly by seabirds and fish, do not reek too
obviously of rot.

Two hours later Elhadj, astoundingly, fishes half a dozen onions out of a red plastic grub bucket and begins to peel them. For
lunch, he says. Soon Djiby kills the motor and in the white and
low winter sun we share the most amazing *ceebu jën* I have ever
had: rice boiled in a spicy broth of onion and bycatch; sliced
murex, crabs, another dead cuttlefish too severely pecked to sell
steaming in the center. At four cardinal points around the seafood, small mounds of diced raw onion with piri-piri pepper and
vinegar bloom like a piquant compass rose.

▼ ▲ ▼

M a Diayi Seck, the mother of Daouda Sarr—pirogue captain, sheep breeder, teller of genii lore—says that when she was a little girl in Palmarin eighty years ago cuttlefish were considered so filthy that parents would not allow their children to eat from the common plate if they had touched one that day. Also back then women would not cook with cymbium and murex. Nor would anyone eat a spooky monkfish, with its toothy hydrocephalic frogface. Fishermen then only fished for tuna or giant African threadfin, sawfish sometimes.

You rarely had to buy fish for everyday lunch. You went to the beach and picked whatever you wanted out of the sea with your hands, like this: you waded into the water and threw an empty rice sack over a school. If you caught too much, you shared it. Sometimes entire schools of sardinella would jump ashore to flee their predators, and then you didn't even have to go into the water. At the time no one thought that one day there would not be enough fish.

Now Ma Diayi's son Daouda is a fisherman. She lives in a yellow room in the clean and spacious house he built two blocks away from the Souarés', helps his two wives take care of the children. Her other son, Mahdi, Daouda's older brother, a soldier, was killed several years ago in a car accident on the road from Mbour. A refrigerator truck owned by a South Korean company that exports frozen mollusk rammed the taxi that was driving him home.

A truck that works for a company owned by white people, Ma Diayi says. A white man's truck.

Ma Diayi unfolds photographs of Mahdi out of carefully creased plastic bags she tucks for safekeeping between bolts of wax print fabric in her cupboard. Her bony hands, hands that never touched cuttlefish, are soft with the shea butter she has been massaging all her life into the skin of her siblings, husband, children, grandchildren. There are other family pictures, color and black and white and sepia. Of her stern-looking late husband with an animal skin draped across one shoulder. Of herself before the children: the pretty, whimsical daughter of a Palmarin *chef du village* who lived to be ninety-six years old. She kneels on the floor of her yellow room, the pictures laid out on the tiled floor before her delicate age-hollowed bones. She is more beautiful now.

She narrates the photographs. Here are Daouda and Mahdi when they were still little. Here is Ma Diayi's mother, the village chief's wife, in an elegant patterned wrap dress, and some of her siblings, monochrome and spunky. Why not all the siblings? Eh, you didn't keep any proof. Proof? Yes. Proof of what? Of the number. Back then white people were in charge and villagers would lie about the number of children in our homes because we were worried that they were looking for soldiers, tirailleurs. White people were always looking for soldiers.

One day, Ma Diayi says, a plane flew and crashed in the bush

near the village. It was before the telephone, people used the tele-
graph then. So the whites in the plane telegraphed for rescue.
Villagers cleared the bush with machetes to help them get out.
But when the white rescuers arrived, the villagers who cleared the
bush became scared. What if the rescuers took them away to be
soldiers? But the village priest came and told the villagers not to
be afraid of the whites. They called him the Priest of Bees, because he had an apiary.

Ma Diayi giggles, and I see that little girl, doing cartwheels on
the beach, picking sardines out of the wrackline with her bare
hands, avoiding cuttlefish, learning to read from nuns. The princess of Palmarin.

She says that when she was little, boats transported peanuts
from the Saloum River port of Foundiougne to Dakar past Palmarin. Sometimes the peanut boats would run aground in the
shoals off the Petite Côte, and the crews would toss the legumes
overboard, like ballast. On such days village kids would fish a
bounty of peanuts out of the swash.

Portuguese colonists brought peanuts to West Africa from
South America in the sixteenth century; after France abolished
slavery, when Ma Diayi's great-grandfather was young, peanuts
and gum arabic replaced the slave trade as Senegambia's most
important export. For the first few years of peanut trade and until
it imposed a peanut import tax to protect its own farmers, the
crop's premier buyer was the United States.

Now Senegal's chief exports are gold and frozen seafood. Yet
peanut remains the main harvest that farmers, by not allowing

the crop to rotate, have turned into a parasitic monoculture, accelerating the degradation of the country's fragile and drought-stricken cultivated land.

I crossed the Saloum River at Foundiougne once, upstream from Palmarin, in the heart of the Peanut Basin. My shared taxi from the border with the Gambia waited for an hour or two to board the northbound ferry. I walked around a bit, stretched my legs. By the crossing women sold dried shrimp in plastic baggies, whole coconut, peanuts: sugared, salted, roasted, raw. A Mouride procession—small boys in front, then men, then women, all young—sang and half-danced past the line of waiting cars to the water and there prayed loudly. The dance was catchy; some travelers joined in. One of my fellow passengers, an imam from Thiès with a hennaed beard, broke a kola nut into asymmetrical lobes and shared it around the battered Peugeot: a eucharist. His wife, a Fulani woman as birdboned and old as Ma Diayi, slid out of the car, took off her green flipflops one by one, knelt by the passenger door, and performed gingerly ablutions with roadside dust. Dipped her dainty fingers in it, touched them to her nose, her forehead, her earlobes. Riverwater rolled softly past a few feet below. On the north side of the river frantic seagulls rose and fell and danced and swarmed over unseen prey.

Seven

Fatou, my landlady's housegirl, has collected her pay and returned to her village inland. Now a neighbor's overzealous daughter, Alima, takes out the slop to dump it in the surf, helps clean fish for the landlady's bistro, wipes the bottoms of the youngest children in the house, carts them around the alley. She may be twelve years old. When Ma Diayi was her age she, too, carried slop to the seashore, carried other women's babies on her back.

One day, slop bucket in hand, Alima spots me at the beach, calls my name, shines upon me her enthusiastic smile. She points: a small child with her skirts hiked is squatting to shit at the wrackline next to a bloated dead she-lamb with an umbilical cord paling about it like a worm. Bad stuff, she says, I cannot tell whether about the defecating child or the dead animal or the serpentine band of multicolored garbage that delineates this day's boundary between land and sea. Or me being there. She secures the slop bucket on her head with her left hand, takes my arm with her right, walks me home.

Sometimes Alima and other preteen girls in my alley get their hands on someone's cellphone and turn up the volume and dance to traditional laments. A Serer goes to sea / goodbye, my love, I will be a fisherman / a Serer goes to sea / goodbye, my love, I will miss you. Their chests not yet female, their giggly gossip and their dance moves already so; fawns. Princesses all, too. Future mothers of fishermen, alive and dead.

▿ ▵ ▿

Khady Diallo, Ndongo's third and youngest wife, in golden lip piercing and catwalk makeup over perfect skin, in Friday robes of blue and yellow eyelet lace and with a pink sequined shawl over her shoulders, on the bare vinyl mattress of Joal hospital's maternity ward. The mattress is brown; the wall tiles are a pattern of pink flowers, the floor tiles are white. There are three wall fans and two doors: to the hospital yard on one side, to the toilet on the side opposite. Khady is curled up on her left side to face the door to the yard. On a cot in the corner a very pregnant schoolgirl in uniform is taking a nap. Someone's leftover IV hangs from a white stand streaked with rust. Ndongo sits at the head of his wife's mattress, picks at a rip in the vinyl. Contractions come every three minutes. This is her second child.

A nurse enters from the yard. A dusty column of morning-sun glare whirls in behind her.

Khady, good morning. You were supposed to be here yesterday.

I was cooking.

Well you're all cooked now.

Khady smiles, then quickly covers her face with her elbow. Draws tighter the shawl. A contraction. Ndongo lets go of the mattress, picks up his wife's purse, opens and closes the kiss clasp. The purse is black faux leather with the word BOSS spelled out in rhinestones. Inside are lipstick, mascara, a cellphone that has run out of credit and that Ndongo is too broke to refill. Opens the clasp, closes. Opens, closes. This is his fourteenth time sitting by a wife in labor. It never gets easier.

The hospital is neat, small brutalist blocks German soldiers built a few years back, beige walls, blue columns, a covered tiled patio, concrete paths. In the shade of the yard outside the pediatric ward, women with quiet infants wait their children's turn for yellow fever shots. At the end of their line a preteen boy squats on the tiles and retches horribly.

Did you go to sea this week? Ndongo asks.

Yes.

With whom?

With Mico Sene's cuttlefish jigger. And with Mamour Ndiaye.

A purse seiner?

Yes.

I see.

When are you going to sea, Ndongo?

I don't know.

Opens the clasp of Khady's purse, closes, opens again.

Maybe tomorrow, inshallah.

It has been a month since Ndongo last went to sea. The construction of the new pirogue has become retrogressive: each day the end seems to sink further away. Whatever Maguette the elder has been catching—on the *Sakhari Souaré*, on the leaking loaner—has been barely enough to cover the price of fuel. There has been no money for wood or nails. Master Ndoye has stopped coming.

The other night Ndongo had this dream:

We are fishing. We have just finished picking net when the pirogue begins to fill with water. She fills and fills. The fish in the bilges rise with the water. You can't stop it. The pirogue begins to founder and we start swimming. Then there is a big sunken ship, an iron ship like the one in Palmarin, and we swim toward her. But whenever we reach our hands to grab her the hull disappears.

Ndongo tells me this dream two days before Khady goes into labor. It is midafternoon; he and I are aboard the dry-docked *Sakhari Souaré*, prepping her for caulking. Ndongo, in flamingo-colored boxers, is taking a break on the bow thwart. Feet dangling, hammer in hand, he watches the sea—white, overexposed in the dry light of late autumn. Unreachable like the iron carcass in his dreams. Draped over the port gunwale his sunbleached jeans are a limp guidon banner of defeat.

I am kneeling amidships, yanking with a pair of pliers old

rusty nails from strips of rubberized industrial hose, the same kind that carries drinking water through Joal. The strips, about four inches wide and three yards long, are to keep the caulking inside the seams; we are reusing the boat's old insulation.

A man approaches, on his way home from the harbor.

Eh, psst! How was the sea today?

Okay.

Got any fish?

Some.

Ndongo has spread a tarp in the net hold and on this tarp he is mixing the caulking emulsion: twenty pounds of cement, ten pounds of mahogany sawdust, baobab leaf powder, tar. The caulking is grainy and sticky and shiny like moist soil. We will stuff it into the long pockets of rubberized hose, which I hammer to the seams inside the pirogue's draft, and nail it shut.

The dry dock has become Ndongo's second home. His two older wives come, bring tea fixings, lunch, children. His seventeen-year-old niece, Aïcha the tomboy, comes to tease and playfight, maybe a bit to flirt. When her affections become too rambunctious Ndongo cuts her off, says: My firstborn would have been older than you if he'd lived.

Alassane's first child. He died at birth, on the way to the hospital. She was in the back of a taxi when he crowned and by the time she arrived he was dead. Her oldest living son is Ousmane. Then Vieux. Then Ousseynou, now nine years old, whose twin brother died in a hospital incubator several days after birth because a nurse had cranked the temperature too high. He cooked in there. The family wanted to sue the nurse for neglect but Fatou Diop Diagne said no, God had willed for him to die. Life is so.

Sokhna, Ndongo's second wife, the mother of Maguette and four other living children, lost only one child. He was eleven days old. The nurses at the Joal hospital did not cauterize his navel properly and it became infected. When the wound began to bleed Sokhna took the baby to the regional hospital in Mbour and waited there for hours for the pediatrician to see him. While they sat in the waiting room the infant bled to death. She was in such a rush to return to Joal to bury him before sundown that she did not ask for the death certificate.

What would that death certificate have said? My tour guide friend's oldest daughter died in infancy several years earlier; as cause of death the doctors at the hospital in Joal wrote, "skin condition." He never tried to investigate what that meant. Children die, he told me. Like most children's graves in the town cemetery, his daughter's is a neat unmarked triangular prism of sand. He visits it once a week, to tidy it up.

Salimata, he tells the sand. Saly.

▽ ▲ ▽

Ndongo was eighteen when he married Alassane, his cousin, the daughter of Fatou Diop Diagne's sister, who lives in Dakar. He tells their love story so:

You know how it is. When you are a young man you want to

try everything, a lot of girls. Your relatives begin to worry that you'll get one of them pregnant. My uncle in Dakar didn't even tell my dad he was getting us married. One day he showed up in Joal with a bag of kola nut. My dad said, What's this? And my uncle said, This is your son and my daughter getting married. Have some kola nut.

They say the first wife is the choice of the parents, the second wife is the choice of the heart, the third wife is the choice of the eye—a trophy wife, the beautiful wife—and the fourth wife is the choice of reason, a child bride who will take care of you when you are old. But Ndongo cannot think of a fourth wife anymore. He must figure out how to support the three he has. Khady remains banned from the Souaré house. He pays her rent and he pays the expenses of all three of his wives and the small children, the ones who do not go fishing yet. Alassane barely makes anything braiding women's hair at the harbor, and Khady, once a fishwife, stopped working soon after she began to show. Sokhna minds the children; her youngest, Moustapha, is six months old. When Sokhna was a schoolgirl in Dakar she wanted to be an athlete, a runner, but her grandmother would not allow that. Women who do sports cannot have children. How will you keep your husband if you do not have children?

How will you keep him if you do? Ndongo's wives click their tongues in sympathy when I explain that I have a son and am divorced. Before I leave town to visit a lover, my landlady, with a wink, hands me a string of black and red bin bin waistbeads and a translucent scarlet wrap to tie around my waist: the traditional

ANNA BADKHEN

182

lingerie of seduction. In my alley two unhappy cousins, Mariama
Thiam and Coumba Ndiaye, suggest that I gain weight to make
myself more attractive, and Coumba brings me costume jewelry.
But mostly they spend their days sitting opposite each other on
low wooden stools, explaining away their own loneliness, the ra-
pacity of their men. Their husbands visited briefly last month for
Tamkharit and then returned to their respective second families—
Mariama's in the Gambia, Coumba's somewhere up north. Mariama is a little older, Coumba and I are the same age. Coumba's
husband took all of their children except for the girl, who now has
a toddler daughter of her own. Mariama lives with her six children, her sole daughter's infant son, and, inexplicably, the three-
year-old daughter of her husband's second wife. Folks on the block
call the girl Gambie.

Sometimes Mariama takes afternoon naps in the alley without
a mat or even a scarf to lay her head on, and then the sand and
seashells and goat droppings and cigarette butts and chicken shit
and peanut husks etch odd designs into the soft skin of her face
and chest and arms. Sometimes she enters the same neighbors'
courtyards five or six times in a single morning, asking the same
people over and over if they slept well, if they are feeling healthy,
wishing them a good day. And sometimes she pulls them aside in
the alley and whispers that she has no money to feed all those
children today, could they please help? But most of the time she
is decorous and calm, and reasons that women in Senegal must be
tolerant of husbands who vanish into polygamy because in this
country there are many more women than men.

It is not true. Only a hundred thousand more women, in a country of fifteen million people. Whence, then, all the second, third, fourth wives? Perhaps they are the abandoned ones, the ones robbed of husbands and fiancés—by philandering spouses, by the sea. I think of Fatou Diop Diagne. Always buying, selling, baking, embroidering bedspreads for sale, playing the lottery the older women of Joal organize each week. You have to hustle: he will have more wives, his attention will shift, he will forget to send money, forget to visit. You must be as inventive as the woman who outwitted Ndiadian Ndiaye.

But Coumba, insomniac, is crying for days on end: her heart, she says, is ripping through her chest. She cannot stand this anymore! She wants a divorce! She storms into my room one day to announce that she has asked for a divorce! "Strip off your pretty clothes, and put on burlap to show your grief, beat your breasts in sorrow," prophesized Isaiah—and in her suffering Coumba parades around the alley naked. Or lures neighbors into her tiny single-room adobe and in that semidarkness moons them, slaps her quavering buttocks, thrusts at them her weedily haired pubis. Her jeweled bin bin, unwanted, wink from between the velvet rolls of her stretchmarked nudity.

▽ ▲ ▽

The *Sakhari Souaré* is now sealed; she will go back to sea in two days, inshallah. The western horizon is black against marmalade sky. A last seagull shrieks. Large bats take the place of birds. Ndongo wipes his hands on the sand, on the jeans he has hung on the boat.

After Amadou ordered Khady out of the house Ndongo wanted to take the rest of his family and leave as well. He even bought some gillnet to start his own fishing business. He was going to work on loaners, or lease a pirogue to own. But his uncle Yoro— Amadou's younger brother, a kind and pigeon-toed master caulker whose only wife is laid up with diabetes in their rented hovel of tin and pirogue board—said that if Ndongo left, people would talk, say that he was disrespectful toward his parents. So he stayed. He added his net to the net of his father.

You know, Anna, he says. In Africa there's a saying that an old man sitting down can see farther than a young man can see standing up. But I think that sometimes a young man can see in his sleep farther than an old man can ever imagine.

He sees the loaner boat sail in. He jumps out of the *Sakhari Souaré* and pulls on his denim pants and strides with a sailor's bowlegged swagger to the shore.

                        ▽ ▲ ▽

Khady gives birth at seven-twenty on a Saturday morning, at halftide on the flood. Ndongo calls my cellphone to tell me the good news:

Anna, come to the hospital! I have a son.

It was an easy birth. At half past eight Khady is sitting up on a cot by the door, eating a pain au chocolat, sipping café Touba from a ceramic mug. Her makeup is gone and she is wearing a multicolored wrap skirt and an oversize white sweatshirt inscribed with the promise LOVE FOREVER AND EVER. The newborn, swaddled in two cotton blankets, is next to her, asleep.

Khady's five-year-old daughter, Sokhna, named after Khady's co-wife, is leaning against the cot on her elbows and letting her bare feet slide backward on the tiles—one, the other, both at once, the favorite game of bored little girls. Khady's mother, who arrived last night from Djifer to help, sails around the room with more coffee, more bread, a banana, some water in a plastic cup. Ndongo slumps on a cot across the room and drums with the edge of his cellphone a nervous rhythm against the metal bedframe. He forces his mouth into a preoccupied smile at my arrival.

Ma'shallah, Khady. *Ma'shallah*, Ndongo. May your new baby have a healthy life full of beauty and happiness.

Amen amen amen.

One more fisherman in the family?

Ha, I guess, says Ndongo.

No way, says Khady.

Ndongo perks up.

No?

Absolutely not.

And why's that?

Khady smiles beautifully at her husband. Takes a bite of her pain au chocolat. Takes a swig from the coffee cup. Takes her time.

She says:

I teased you. It's a girl. I've known for months from the ultrasound that it was going to be a girl.

Ndongo rises, crosses the room to his wife's cot, unswaddles the bottom of the newborn's blankets, peeks in. Khady laughs hard, nearly spills coffee in her lap. Ndongo laughs, too. Fooled by a woman, again. Sokhna, confused, looks from one parent to another then laughs as well because it is something new to do. Her grandmother chuckles, sits down, takes the girl by the hand, drags her into the hammock of skirts between her knees, rocks her there, slaps her shoulders lightly as she speaks. Tap tap tap.

The gender is not important, she says. Tap tap tap. What is important is that the child—boy or girl—have *baraka*, the blessing of God. That's what really matters.

Tap tap tap. The grandmother sways and the girl sways within her embrace. Khady picks up the baby, gives her the nipple, sways also. Three generations of mothers and future mothers rocking this way, rocking that way, keeping rhythm with the sea.

Now you are a big sister, the old woman chants. You will be wise. Sometimes you will carry the baby on your back. Sometimes you will wash her. When you carry her on your back you have to be careful not to fall. Tap tap tap. See? Anna is writing everything down. That means everything I say is true.

And Ndongo, laughing, says, Amen. He reaches to caress Sokhna's knobby back, plays with her vertebrae. One two three four five and down four three two one. Floats on a headrope. He winks at his wife.

Remember? When you were giving birth to this one you screamed a lot.

No I didn't! But with this one—she nods at the swaddles at her breast—I really screamed with this one, wallahi! This stubborn baby with her big head.

Women file into the doorway, utter a litany of blessings. Friends, neighbors, distant relatives. They bring baby soap, laundry soap, talcum powder: gold, frankincense, myrrh. Khady and her mother singsong greetings and gratitudes. No one from Ndongo's side of the family comes. Fatou Diop Diagne does not visit the hospital nor Khady's house to greet her new granddaughter. She does not make an offering of sweet *lakh* to the genie who has the power to protect or punish the women in her bloodline.

It's because of Khady's haughtiness, she tells me later at the Souaré house over sweet mint tea. The tea makes my mouth taste like a garden. Khady should be more humble, act more like Alassane and Sokhna, Ndongo's first two wives. The baby, she says, will have to do without the sacrifice.

Will this cause problems for the baby?

Eh! Who knows? Here we are, together, drinking tea. Perhaps the baby will not have any problems.

▽ ▲ ▽

Ndongo acknowledges the visitors by clicking his cellphone against the cotframe and humming. Mm. Mm. Mm. He is rocking, too. Tallying up expenses in his head.

The fifty-dollar hospital bill for delivery and vaccinations. Traditional new mother's meals for Khady for the first week—boiled millet flour with sugar, bananas, soup with meat in it, rice with peanut sauce and sugar. Vitamins for Khady. Diapers. And a week from today he must hold a naming ceremony for the baby. He must pay for a sacrificial sheep and rice and a griot and musicians and a beautician for Khady and matching outfits for her best friends, or else he will not be able to invite friends whose blessings will bring the girl *baraka*, bring her luck.

Oh, God, how will he pay for all of this? There is no money. And there are no fish. A big pirogue like the one Master Ndoye has been building can carry a lot of fuel and go fishing far from shore, where the haul is more likely to be good. But the big pirogue is nowhere near done. She is missing sheers, thwarts, gunwales, splashboard, lazarette, motor well, counter, boomkin. A small pirogue like the *Sakhari Souaré* must stay close to shore. But there are no fish close to shore.

Wallahi, Anna, I really don't know how I will manage.

Wisps of opera arias carry from the nurses' station, where hospital guards are drinking sweet tea and listening to the radio.

Morning light casts a rectangle of bright white onto the white tiles of the ward floor through the half-open door. Ndongo stares at the rectangle with his faraway sea captain's eyes. He did not sleep at all last night.

▽ ▲ ▽

Anurse discharges Khady and the baby at ten-thirty in the morning, three hours after birth. Khady goes to the bathroom to wash up and her mother produces from someplace a soapy rag and quickly wipes the bloody lochia stain off the mattress. Mamma spilled some coffee, she tells Sokhna, who is watching. Grandmother tricks. We learn them not from mothering our own children but afterward somehow, in some unconscious leisurely reflection, and we arrive armed with such wisdoms to receive the children we will not need to raise. Quick little lies, quick little comforts. On occasion my neighbor Mariama Thiam suckles her infant grandson with her own long-empty breast to quiet him to sleep.

They file out of the maternity ward: Khady and the baby, Khady's mother, Sokhna. Ndongo follows with Khady's bag of yesterday's clothes in one hand and a bucket with a teapot and cups and unfinished baguettes in the other. He leaves his women to wait with the bags in the shade of the hospital wall and steps into the asphalt road to flag a taxi. In the middle of Boulevard Jean Baptiste Collin, Captain Ndongo Souaré raises both arms high in the air like a man desperate, pleading for some fundamental deliverance.

He pays the driver in advance, holds the cab doors open for the women. He does not go with them. He stands in the road, blinking at the bright light, then sets out, on foot, for the wharves.

There is no one at the graving dock. No one at Mbaar Kanené, or at Mbaar Atelier Taïf. The *Sakhari Souaré* is out fishing with Maguette at the helm. Ndongo's uncle Yoro is caulking the outside seams of someone's pursenetter with a greenish paste of sawdust, whiting, paint thinner, crushed styrofoam, and baobab powder. The elastic mixture looks like rising yeast dough, like something you would want to put in your mouth. Ndongo pushes himself up onto the gunwale of a nearby jigger. Swings his legs to heel the hull. Maybe tomorrow he will go to sea. Depends on what they catch today. Inshallah. Inshallah.

That evening from the north a wonder: a cool sustained wind, and out-of-season raindrops, which I mistake at first for crickets.

▽ ▲ ▽

W ho can say if there will be fish for him when Ndongo finally returns to sea? Of the hundred and forty-seven species of marine creatures fished off Senegal's coast, fifty-one are threatened. In the last fifty years, a fifth of all fish stocks have become overexploited. Half of the fish stocks have collapsed.

That week I watch the forty-footer *Yaye Khodia Dieng* cast an eight-hundred-foot purse seine in six spots in the marine sanctuary under the supervision of the sanctuary's volunteer president, Karim Sall, who is also my landlord, and three rangers. The pirogue delivers her haul to a *mbaar* in the center of town, behind the old marketplace, where reserve employees and volunteers weigh each specimen on a toploading scale or a spring scale and measure them with a soft tape measure and consult a bilingual tome of *The Fresh and Brackish Water Fishes of West Africa, Vol. II,* to log them in a journal. Senegal's seven marine protected areas have been inventorying their fisheries this way every six months for the last decade. This is how they track the ocean's slow decline.

The *Yaye Khodia Dieng,* with PARIS SAINT-GERMAIN and ILA TOUBA inscribed upon her green hull in immoderate rococo calligraphy, belongs to Baye Geye, an old retired fisherman with cataractic eyes who moved to Joal from Saint-Louis in 1971 and lives in a large walled compound near the harbor, right next to Mbaar Kanené. Her crew are Captain Malick Seye and his six teenage nephews. Malick is the brother of one of Baye's wives and Ndongo Souaré's distant cousin.

Fishermen often moonlight for the conservancy, though they poach the reserve incessantly and openly and though the underpaid rangers habitually confiscate and resell the fishers' catch they deem unlawful. Disputes between poachers and corrupt rangers come to blows sometimes. But in a small town all transgressions and offenses are out in the open and are easy to put aside when a day's work for the reserve promises a paycheck for the entire crew. After all, the fishers are not snitching, like some. Snitching is a trespass unpardonable, punished by magic.

The pirogue casts twice in the Mama Nguedj, then twice along the shore of Palmarin, and twice more within sight of Joal's ruffled shore. Boys sing their hauling shanties—

What's your name?—motherfucker!—what's your name?—motherfucker!—

and

Haul the rope!—I want to feel you—haul the rope!—I want to feel you—haul the rope!—

and

If you eat a kilo of meat—there will be oil in your shit!—

and haul a few handfuls of tiny adolescent fish. They haul a juvenile green sea turtle, maybe two feet long; then four more, twice as large. Their rubbery flippers and necks are pale and barnacles jag where the scutes seam the enormous dark olive teardrops of their veined and marbled carapaces. One turtle clenches unchewed bright seagrass in its serrated beak, stunned to be caught midmeal. The Triassic reptiles take up the entire midships. Boys turn them upside down to stop them crawling and stand on their smooth yellow plastrons to pose for cellphone pictures. Impersonate the world that rests upon a tortoise. Are that world.

A green sea turtle can weigh seven hundred pounds, measure five feet in length, spend several hours underwater without breathing, and may travel sixteen hundred miles from its grazing sites to breed, navigating by sunlight, wave direction, water temperature, and the magnetic field of the Earth. Adult green turtles are herbivores and live up to a hundred years in the wild. It takes them between twenty and fifty years to reach sexual maturity, the longest of all marine turtles; only one out of a hundred makes it to reproductive age. Polyandry is rare. A female lays about a hundred eggs per clutch every two years and buries them in sand at night; the eggs hatch about two months later, also at night, and the hatchlings—soft-bodied and almost black and no larger than an avocado pit—crawl seaward by instinct, by genetic memory.

A green turtle can mate for seventy-two hours. You can acquire some of that stamina if you steep a turtle penis in hot water like tea and drink the infusion. Then you can maintain an erection all night long.

I've tried it, one of the sanctuary's rangers tells me. It works very well.

An average green turtle penis is twelve inches long but drinking the infusion will not affect the size of your own penis.

Ah! says Karim, my landlord. Having a long penis is not very useful.

Karim is forty-nine, a retired fisherman. He is the volunteer president of the conservancy and of Senegal's largest artisanal fishermen's union, an occasional paid lecturer on mangrove conservation and marine protection, a husband of two wives and father of six children, a breeder of sheep and pigeons, and a loquacious know-it-all. He begins:

When you get old it doesn't stay hard, that's why—

—you have a short penis? I guess.

We laugh.

No-o-o, that's why women look for younger lovers, Karim says. But it's okay to have a medium-size penis.

Fulani herders give the turtle penis extract to their inseminator bulls. If you cut the single claw off the turtle's flipper and hang it from an infant's neck the baby will start walking sooner. Green turtle meat and calipee are part of the traditional coastal diet along Senegal's coast. Turtle is more tender than beef, sweeter.

Can we keep one? Captain Malick asks a ranger.

No you cannot. We will weigh them, measure them, tag them, and release them.

But just one?

No.

Oh, come on. It's been a while since we've had turtle meat.

The *Yaye Khodia Dieng* is almost to the *mbaar* when one of the teenage deckies squats down beside the largest turtle, squints at it—and suddenly and with all his might punches its leathery helmeted head. The turtle flinches mightily, paddles its useless upside-down flippers in the air. The boy sucks his teeth, hits it again. Unleashes some primal viciousness. One Leviathan against another.

▽ ▲ ▽

Sometimes male turtles are so exhausted by coitus they slip off their mates' shells and drown.

⛢ ⛢ ⛢

Once, on my sunrise run through the mangroves, I happened upon a group of men butchering a green turtle with axes and machetes behind the white shell cemetery midden near Fadiouth. The carapace was gone. There were two small piles of thick white skin and connective tissue and the men were chopping at the amorphous mound of bloody meat and lumps of bright green fat upon a black plastic tarp.

⛢ ⛢ ⛢

All transgressions in a small town are out in the open: every fisherman knows who the town snitch is. He spends his days at the same *mbaar* where sanctuary employees inventory their test catch. Fishermen say he has two ways of making a living: by telling them when it is safe to cast in the sanctuary—and by telling on them, informing the rangers. They say he makes a hundred dollars a pop either way. Trouble starts when he double-dips.

The week he tells the *Mansor Sakho* that it is okay to fish in the reserve and then rats her out so she gets caught with bilges full of sanctuary catfish and has to pay nearly a thousand dollars in fines—that week the pirogue's crew lie on the floor in one of the blue-walled rooms of Captain Mamour Ndiaye's house and chain-smoke cigarettes and weed and plot revenge. Mamour, naked from the waist up as usual, does most of the talking.

I will tell you this, he says. This is Africa. We have black magic here. And here, if you use the money you got by harming others to feed your family, then one day maybe one of your family members will die from eating that food.

Amen, say the men.

Just wait and see, says Mamour. Bad things will happen to this man. I have powers. If you destroy something of mine, next year I will destroy something of yours.

Amen, say the men.

The informer was a fisherman himself once, says Mamour's brother Moustapha. Then some of the fishermen he had screwed became so exasperated they cast a spell on him. Cursed him away from water. Now, if one of his feet touches the sea, it becomes bloated.

Yeah, and if he doesn't watch it, says Mamour, he may go blind.

Smoke pours out of his mouth and nostrils and churns below the yellow rings of dried rainwater on the canvas ceiling.

∇ ∆ ∇

Later I stop by the *mbaar*. The man is there, watching young fishers play football in the sand. His back is to the cerulean sea. His left foot is bare. His right is sheathed in a black ankle sock.

⚐ ▲ ⚐

You name a baby after someone you love, whose presence and spirit will safeguard the child, will guide the child to become successful, strong, lucky. You name one son Papa after your own father and another son after your best friend Papa; everyone in the family will know the difference. My landlord, Karim, named his eldest daughter Mah after his mother; he named his third daughter Mah after the girl's mother, his first wife. A fisherman friend is named Abou after a tirailleur soldier who had served in the Korean War, but one of his brothers is named Abou after someone else; to tell them apart, folks call my friend Abou Korea.

Or you name a baby to trick evil spirits, to ward off the evil eye. Amoul Yakar—Without Hope—is a child born after several stillbirths. Bougouma—I Don't Want You—is a girl born after all her older siblings have died. A family's tragic history outlined and locked into the name a child will bear forever. Along with our parental expectations, our fears, our hopes, our projections, and our failures, from birth and for the rest of his or her life, amen.

Naming is a morning ritual. Early on the seventh day of the baby's life elders gather. The father whispers the desired name to the imam, who holds it inside his mouth, safeguards it like a shiny blue bead until the time comes. In the mother's bedroom, older women arrive in an unhurried procession of long brocade boubous and with matching wallets of faux crocodile skin, of

patent leather, of beaded velvet. They bring money for the mother
and soap for the baby. They shuck their sequined sandals by the
door and sit heavily on the embroidered bedspread of the huge
matrimonial bed and on as many plastic chairs as can crowd
around it. They sip some café Touba, nibble on some pain au
chocolat. Then, in the room heavy with their perfume and their
pomp, they pick up the baby, dressed in a white and pink onesie
that reads SWEETHEART on the chest and LOVE on each of the
soles, and take turns shaving her head with a razor blade. They
shift the infant this way and that, squeeze her between their
knees, lay her across their laps, vertically, upside-down, sideways.
They pinch the blade between forefinger and thumb, keep their
pinkies delicately extended. A calabash to catch the soundless soft
black ringlets. They pass them around, the baby and the blade
and the calabash, the baby always first. They work thoroughly
and without rushing and talk softly about childbirth: theirs, their
daughters', their sisters', their friends'. The only light comes from
the dull rectangle of the door draped with lavender gauze, and
each time a new guest stands in the threshold for long *salaams*
she blocks out the light and the women shave the baby in redolent
darkness.

When the newborn's head is shaved completely smooth, the
women add to the calabash with her hair a pinch of millet, so she
may never go hungry; a shred of cottonwool, so she may always
have clothes on her back; a splash of water, so she may never know
thirst; and a kola nut, to bring her luck. Then one of them takes
the calabash out to the street, where men suck on hard ginger

candy and talk about fishing. The men take turns peeking inside the calabash to ascertain its contents and add the final ingredient of the baby's future happiness: money. Then the women file out of the room and sit with the men to pray. At the end of the prayer the imam says the name he has been guarding all morning, the name that will protect and honor the child in this life and in the life after.

Ndeye Khady: Mamma Khady. Mamma's little girl.

▽ ▲ ▽

Three hours later, Khady Diallo, in eyelash and nail extensions, gets her hair done in front of a large bedroom mirror decorated with her strings of bin bin waistbeads and her wedding photographs faded to red and pink. A tailor delivers a set of six matching orange and blue brocade dresses for her six closest girlfriends, who primp at Khady's vanity table stacked with bottles of deodorant and hair spray. Outside, Vieux Sene and Gora Sall, whose wife Mariama Boye sells breakfast at Mbaar Atelier Taïf, lug to the roof a hundred pounds of rice, mounds of onions and carrots and turnip for the sauce, and two heavy cans of propane to cook it all, then set up two tarps—one on the roof, for the makeshift kitchen, one in the sandfilled street, for the guests. Older women upstairs instantly set to peeling and dicing. Ndongo unties the sacrificial sheep from the sardine-grade fishnet where children from the block tormented it all morning and drags it to the roof, where he slaughters it inexpertly while the women look away. Flies stick to the dark bloodstain. Boys fetch and arrange under and around the tarp the same borrowed battery of enumerated white and blue plastic chairs that attends all of Joal's life events. Here in the afternoon several dozen women in lowcut mermaid dresses of rich brocade and lace will fan themselves, untie the infants from their backs, let their hips swing.

By five o'clock an unbroken and ageless drumbeat pumps through giant loudspeakers, floods Joal's Santhie Deux district, the neighborhood of immigrant fishers nearest the harbor. In a corner of the party tent four drummers spray sweat. Fronting them a wormy griot in skinny jeans and a tanktop is debauching the women.

Madames! Madames! Dance of the First Wife!

Whack! go the drums, and first wives step into the arena, whirl, gyrate, slap one another's bejeweled palms.

The first wife is wise / she knows all of her husband's desires / she knows how to please him / and obey his parents!

Hell yeah! Jumping squats and pirouettes and outthrust hips in swags of flying sand and cheeks blush with sparkling rouge and sweat and cheers and laughter and the griot motions for the band to up the speed and announces the more frenzied—

Madames! Dance of the Second Wife!

Whack! Whack! go the drums.

The first wife is old / she can't remember anything / the second wife is much nicer / and far more beautiful!

And the second wives, barefoot and in inches of gold bracelets and towering headdresses and makeup, twerk and giggle, make to rub against the griot, against one another, against the tall djembe goblet drums—

Ladies! Ladies, the Ass Dance!

Yeah!

Who took the chair? / Who, who took the chair? / Show us how you go down baby / Shake that ass like this, roll it like this / Who took the chair?

And the dancers jump into the sandy arena under the tent alone and in pairs and threes, and kick up dust and perfume, and ululate and twist and toss toss toss their brightly wrapped buttocks high in the air, and thrust their breasts at the griot and his drummers, legs and arms akimbo until their clothes unravel, wigs and turbans fly off, a raunchy hurricane of violet and scarlet and indigo and silver and gold, a tempest of womanhood, the fishwives' ecstasy this time for no one's pleasure but their own—though from the shade across the street men in seated rows tap one another's forearms politely to get a better view of the clamorous rainbow erupting under the tent.

And shake it shake it shake it yeah!

Okay, ladies! And now! Get down for! Dance! Of the Third! Wife!

Whack! Whack! Whack!

And to a drumroll Khady sails into the heart of the celebration in a long dress of black and silver gauze and fake diamond earrings down to her shoulders and a silver clutch and matching spike heels. She smiles, lets the griot hold her by the waist, lets him hold the microphone to her lipsticked mouth.

Who makes you happy, Khady?

Ndongo!

What? Who makes you happy, Khady?

Ndongo!

Who? I can't hear!

Ndongo!

Louder, girl, who? I still can't hear!

Ndongo-Ndongo-Ndongo!

Khady crosses the street to the row of chairs where her husband sits with his friends. Her heels sink through the sand. Glittering with makeup she leans down, kisses Ndongo on the cheek in front of the cheering crowd. The captain breaks a sweat. She plops into his lap to pose for pictures, directs his hand to her waist. He squeezes deeper into his chair, as if it could corkscrew down through the unpaved street and reappear aboard a pirogue where he can set wide his sea legs, be tough, be confident, be in charge.

Ndongo's mother and his first and second wives, Alassane and Sokhna, are invited to the celebration. They do not come.

▽ ▲ ▽

As the sun drops, the naming-day guests leave, the musicians pack up, wind calms, waves quiet. In the flat silver water under the flat silver sky a fisherman pays out his seine, now ankle-deep, now thigh-deep in flow tide. The shore: the Earth's exposed shoulderblade. Stirred by the moon, the sun, the farthest star in the universe, set in motion by cosmic powers, the ocean wipes it clean each day twice.

By the time the fisherman hauls his seine, the sea erases into the dark. A heavy African night falls.

In Khady's rented room, hairless and blessed, the newborn sleeps alone at the edge of her mother's bed.

v ▲ v

Fishermen at the *mbaar* tell a story of a woman who used to work on pirogues.

She worked well, says Coura Kane.

She could outwork any lazy man, says Ndongo.

Wallahi, that girl! When she went out to sea with her brothers and her oldest brother couldn't come, she would be captain for that day, says Vieux.

Where is this woman? Can I meet her? The men shrug. Been a long time. Maybe she is married now. Yes, maybe in some other town. The she-captain is more elusive than the genii. A slippery, free waterspirit. For all the rocking in their mother's arms Khady Diallo's daughters will never know the ocean's rise and pitch. The women who are flesh and blood, the ones with whom I drink tea and cook and gossip and bargain over vegetables, are the humble ones, the ones who remain ashore, like my neighbors Mariama Thiam and Coumba Ndiaye; like Action's mother, Marie Badiane;

like Captain Mamour's wife Yacine, waiting by the sea for uncer-
tain returns. Like the woman I pass on one of my twilit walks
home along the wrackline. She has brought her three children to
sit with her on the dirty sand under a large pursenetter. In an
immobile row they face the Atlantic. One child to her left, two
smaller ones to her right, huddled inside her single transparent
lavender shawl. Waiting, waiting. Penelopes, the tribe of ancient
sea widows.

I keep forgetting that I, too, am a woman at the mercy of men.

After so many years trying to affect an observer's detachment
from my hosts I have grown to believe in my separateness: that I
am a benign interloper for whom patriarchies make exceptions,
almost invisible to the people who entrust me with their stories,
excluded from the aspects of life related to love or sex—even
spared, up to a point, by warring armies, though not by grief.
Keeping apart is often lonely, but it also feels professional, emo-
tionally safe. It is a foolish and unrealistic endeavor. In Joal, as in
the world, our lives leach into one another constantly. My landlady's three-year-old son demands that I give him his afternoon
baths. Apparently I sudse well. Children in the alley have begun
to call me Auntie. Despite myself my carefully calibrated distance
recedes with each trip to sea, each night ashore worrying about a
boat that is running late.

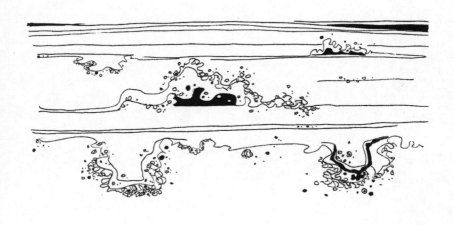

Eight

White sky, white sea, and no horizon. It has been like this for a week. December dust is settling in. Dawns seem delayed. Beneath white clouds the reef egrets spooked out of the mangrove marsh fly blue. The gurgling of herons in a kapok tree like clatter of bones, like a death rattle. The stagnant pools of summer rainwater have become concave football pitches where boys kick balls with bare feet. Baked rot rims them limegreen.

The night-fishing season has begun and Magal Touba has finished but no pirogues go out: the waxing moon has kicked up waves and scattered the fish. Now not Ndongo alone but all of Joal's fishermen pace the shore with the unsettled groinache of young lovers. Kedge anchor rodes that parcel out the beach dance up and down, taut and slack with the nodding sterns of their pirogues. Umbilicals. The shore is so dry that at night my blanket and mosquito net sparkle each time I shift.

▽ ▲ ▽

Where the money came from, Ndongo would not say. But after the naming ceremony Master Ndoye returns from Mbour to finish building the pirogue. He carvel-planks the sheers and ratchets them in place and hammers the slender inwales alongside them like ellipses. He secures the boat's curves with nine thwarts, knees the thwarts to the hull, removes the ratchet strap. Builds footholds in the bilge under each thwart. Finds the sturdiest strips of recycled mahogany still palimpsested with the scoffed paint job of the old *Ndaye Adja Kane*, kerfs them into gunwhales, nails those in. Circles the pirogue often: clockwise, counterclockwise, shuts one eye then another to check for symmetry. Anna, hammer. Anna, nails. Anna, hold. The mahogany is heavy, splintery; against its warm weight and the shipwright's incantatory orders I am not an apprentice but merely a tool. Master Ndoye nails in the risers port and starboard, fortifies the boomkin with two knee joints, lowers a splashboard into place above the lazarette. On the last day he walks up to the keel and backs out his semioval signature stamp into the bowsprit port and starboard: his whiskey plank. Then Ndongo comes and plugs a fist-size gap in a board with a flipflop.

Together Yoro and I caulk the seams. Ndongo paints the bow red and white and green, the stern green, the hull below the waterline brown, the topside white. He paints the ceiling brown and the waterline black. Ousmane paints the middle of the thwarts

the palest blue, nails rectangles of multifilament net from thwarts'
bottoms to thwart risers to portion out holds. I paint the gunwales and the top of the transom scarlet. The bitt, where the
mooring lines get wound—red at the bottom, yellow in the middle, green at the top, the colors of the Senegalese flag—is misshapen, jagged, perhaps to offer easier grip to those crew who
watch for fish on the prow. Or to approximate the rostrum of a
sawfish, that ancient totem of strength that has been fished out to
near extinction. Ndongo does not know for sure. It's just how
we've always done it, he says.

The next afternoon the artist Moustapha Faye arrives at the dry
dock in splattered denim jeans and a tee shirt. He paints a design
of three lobed green leaves in the middle of the hull on each side.
He shadows the leaves canary yellow. He draws red arabesques
like claws streaming downward from the leaves. He paints a pair
of red-tipped green and black spears in the stern. In the middle of
the hull he spells the new boat's name in black.

On the starboard side: SAKHARI SOIRE. On the port: SOIRE
SAKHARI. Inside each letter *O*, a white star.

An alternative spelling, I say.

It's a proper name, we spell it however we like, says Ndongo.

If they spelled it the other way, with the *o-u-a*, there would
have been no room for the red part of the design, says Vieux.

Amadou Souaré says:

Her license will say *"Sakhari Soiré*, sixteen meters," with an *i*.

He squats and writes in the sand with his thick index finger, in Arabic, *ma'shallah*; says: Once the artist is finished painting the hull I will give him this word to write inside. To protect against envy. And the letter *waw*. To help the pirogue leave and return safely.

Amadou is in a good mood. His new pirogue is almost ready to sail. And a week earlier he went to Kaolak and finally married the woman he had been pining for.

The late December sunset is deep orange and the low cloud on the horizon is dusty lavender, the sky above it pale yellow then pale blue. The moon overhead is almost full. The sea is an uninterrupted sheet of gold. Upon it flocks of birds: pelicans, seagulls. A pod of pelicans stretches from a vee into a straight line and flies low and coils above the water and then lifts unevenly like a snake about to sting and lowers again and finally rests on the water in a constellation of black dots. We watch it. At a nearby church, in French and off-key, children practice carols about Jesus and chocolate. The beat is vehement, a hallelujah.

▽ ▲ ▽

O n the morning of the winter solstice the sun rises late over low tide. Gilded water, cool northeast wind. Silver breakers six feet tall. Boats roll this way, roll that. Boats anchored and not kedged whorl about the anchorlines, facing to sea, facing to shore. At Mbaar Kanené, Ndongo in a tattered and paint-splotched blue gym suit mends net. He grins at me, winks with a bloodshot eye.

The artist is almost done with
the big pirogue, he says. We'll
put her in the water after
lunch, inshallah. Today, today,
yes. Go take a look.

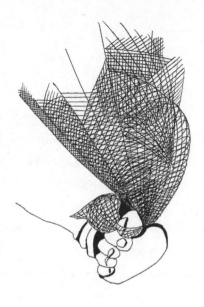

I approach the *Sakhari Soiré*
on port. The artist Moustapha
Faye has been at the graving
dock since dawn. He has
spelled the boat's license number in white on the green field
of the bow: TI-0725JL. He
has painted a blue stripe under
her red gunwale. He has—

Below the blue, close to the
stern, where captains ask artists to write *Paris Saint-Germaine* or
Lionel Messi or the name of their favorite wrestler, Moustapha has
spelled my name.

Too late I recognize the one boundary I hold inviolate, unques-
tionable: the protective shell of a storyteller, my perceived immu-
nity as one who passes through. I discover and identify it the very
moment it is erased, dismissed, written over. The breach pierces,
humbles, bewilders, triggers the topsy-turvy familiarity of *mal de
débarquement*. I am no longer a storyteller. I am a mascot. When
the *Sakhari Soiré* sets sail she will take me with her everywhere
she goes.

▽ ▲ ▽

On the afternoon of the winter solstice, at perigee high tide, forty-three men and boys put the *Sakhari Soiré* in the sea.

Amadou Souaré is the first to the dry dock. In a white boubou with large red polkadots and a pair of large sunglasses he stands facing his new pirogue bowlegged, feet apart. Between his feet in the sand lies a meaty chunk of tuna belly with flesh the same color as the polkadots, a donation from a younger fisherman back from a trip. He stands above the bleeding hunk unmoving in his flowing dress, a seedy Neptune. He waits.

The *Sakhari Soiré* rests on two palm logs. Gone are the sandbag and the brace of painted pirogue boards. Gone are the nails and the sawdust: this morning Ndongo and his halfbrothers swept her clean, brushing first from the bow toward center hold, then from the stern toward center hold, because center hold is where the fish and the net will be, God willing. Beside her starboard transom lie a four-fluke anchor the size of a small cow and a rudder eight feet long. The rudder is soldered from black new-looking stock and a rusted, seaworn iron tiller. Which pirogues has it steered through the Atlantic before, over which depths has it beaded bright waters into necklets of wake, on which quests has it ferried the sea's spellbound disciples?

I stand on tiptoe on a palm log and push myself up to peek inside the boat. Gora Sall says a few years back there was a gill-netter that caught so many fish she was drawing water overboard.

Gora says such a thing will never happen again: not enough fish. Still I try. I see fish in the brand-new holds of the pirogue I helped build. I imagine its smell, the slippery, slapping mess of it all the way up to the pale-blue thwarts. As if such seeing can conjure it up. My arms tire. The pirogue is empty. She reeks of paint thinner.

Yoro Souaré arrives in a boubou cut from the same polkadot cloth as his brother's. He worries a string of prayer beads in his left hand and fists a green ball of caulk in his right. He walks around the *Sakhari Soiré*, inspects her one last time. His intoeing forces him to bend at the waist. To bow to the pirogue. Now and then he stops to smear sealant over exposed nails so salt does not rust them. When Ndongo comes, Yoro fishes out of a pant pocket an amulet wrapped in plastic and tied with twine.

Here, son. May God help you sail out safely and return in peace.

Amen.

Ndongo shucks his flipflops, climbs into the pirogue, hammers a nail in the chain locker, hangs the gris-gris from it. Hops aft on bare feet from thwart to thwart to secure at the transom a gudgeon for the rudder. Then fleets fore again and from the prow summons his friends.

Psst! Eh! Come, let's launch this boat!

Fishermen shuffle over, complaining. The wheelbarrow is much too small to hoist the boat on it. There are not enough palm logs to help roll her to the sea. There is no fish in the sea anyway. Some fishermen are eating rice and beans! Many have

been going to the Gambia to catch something, but prices in the Gambia are low. A fisherman says, One of my friends says this prayer before going to sea: "May God separate me from this boat," because fishing is hard and it would be better to find a different job.

On the prow Ndongo sucks his teeth. Shut up. Let's do it. Let's launch 'er, for God's sake.

They lodge the wheelbarrow under the boat's keel at the bow and gather at the stern and begin to push fifty-two feet of mahogany toward cold chop the color of steel. They roll her over her two supporting logs and they stop to grab the log she has rolled over and shove it under her keel at the fore again. Then the other log. Then the wheelbarrow. Repeat. They slide bits of sheetmetal and plastic and tarp under the wheels when the wheelbarrow sinks too deeply into sand dry and loose as silt. Pushing, pulling, yelling, sweating, cursing. The pirogue creaks, inches forward, stops, moves again. They call out, Hey, men, strength strength! and they keep count of this call because before the *Sakhari Soiré* hits water they must repeat it exactly thirty-three times—the eternal age of all dwellers of heaven; the exact number of angels who carry man's praise to God; the age of Issa on the cross; the symbol of the Seal of Solomon; the sum of beads in each of the three sets of a trisected rosary that, counted together, correspond to the entire ninety-nine names of God of which the thirty-third is al Azim, the Incomparably Great.

In the bow by the bitt Ndongo stands like a figurehead.

Take out the log!

Come over to port!

Hold up, hold up!

Like men now, like men!

Hey, men, strength strength!

The boat seesaws on the small wheelbarrow. Up and down on pretend waves. Tests that oscillation that will be hers for as long as she lasts in the sea. She barely clears the gap on the shore between a large purse seiner dry-docked for a paint job and two small abachi trapsetters, and Yoro motions for some men to lift these light boats and move them out of the way. Inside the stern of one, between the name of Muhammad spelled in Arabic and the letter *waw* written seven times, the owner has hung a toddler's canvas left shoe, the way taxi drivers dangle them from a rear bumper, or horsecart owners nail them to their carts. A gris-gris. When the men lift the pirogue the shoe swings and a used condom sails out of the midships, a glimpse into the secret life of beached pirogues. You hang your laundry between them to dry, you fuck your boyfriend in their holds, you sit in their shade and watch the sea for your husband returning, not returning. In their hereafter they become benches, door fragments, pillars, fences, gates, new boats.

The procession is almost to the tideline when Ndongo's half-brothers hoist the anchor above their heads and hand it to him and he drops it into the chain locker. The pirogue launches without an outboard.

Hey, men, strength strength!

Her bow hits the water first. A shattering of diamonds spouts skyward in a brilliant crown. She teeters on the feeble pushcart, which is now stuck in silt and seaweed, slides off it on her beam ends, almost hits the *Sakhari Souaré,* her little older sister whose six wooden thwarts are festooned with net. Steadies, to cheers from the shore. Ndongo's nine-year-old son, Ousseynou, the twin whose brother was killed by a hospital nurse, strips and darts into the cold ocean to swim the wheelbarrow ashore. On the prow Ndongo, drenched in surf, grips a hawser in his hands like reins and rides his father's chariot boat into the Atlantic.

▽ ▲ ▽

Silver sun, silver sky, sea like molten steel. Fishermen along the wrackline in a line of their own face the ocean. There, Ousmane Souaré and his teenage uncle Saliou are swimming over to the new pirogue, now anchored about a hundred feet offshore. A bobbing white dot in Ousmane's outstretched hands: a bucket full of milk. An oblation.

Amadou Souaré narrates Ousmane's passage:

Many years ago fishermen in Senegal were heathen and did not know proper Muslim prayers to bless pirogues, to protect their homes and safeguard their loved ones. So instead of asking God they asked genii to bless and protect. Because God is merciful he accepted these rituals—not all of them, but some. Those were the rituals they kept after converting. For example, I know a prayer that will protect you from a snake's venom.

Even if a lion bites you that prayer will protect you, says Pa Ousmane Sall.

Yes, I know both kinds of protection prayer. And Fatou, my first wife, she has a special connection with the genii. The kind of sacrifice a genie asks for is usually milk. So when we have a new boat she prepares milk, and we pour this milk inside the pirogue from the stern to the bow on the starboard side, then from the bow to the stern on the port side, then from the stern to the bow along the middle. What Ousmane and Saliou are doing now.

Except they are stupid, says Captain Malick Seye. Look! They just put the blessing in the pirogue and now they are bailing it out. Eh! Psst! Stop bailing!

Stop bailing, stop bailing, eh! shouts Yoro Souaré. He squints at the boat bobbing in the sea that shines mercilessly, a pulsating glint that cuts the eye. Look how high she rides, he says. They'll have to put ten bags of sand in the stern so that the motor touches water.

A fisherman walks by with a broom of Sodom's apple in a plastic bag—to shield from the dark magic some other pirogue, or a house, or a newborn baby. He stops, shakes hands with the fishermen, utters a blessing for the *Sakhari Soiré*. A fishwife on her way to harbor says, May the new boat be strong. The steep seas heave the moored pirogues, toss them about their anchorage, clank one against another. The whole shoreline rattles, groans as wood slams and rubs against wood. Past the yo-yoing boats Ndongo swims from the *Sakhari Soiré* to the shore in his ripped blue gym suit, straightens up waist-deep in loud surf, comes ashore dripping, beaming.

Boats should use both a kedge and an anchor in such waves, Malick says.

Yes, these waves are too strong, Gora says.

People always should have a kedge anchor or two aboard, in case they lose the main anchor in the wind.

Yes—did you see that boat from Mbour? She only had one anchor. Such a shame, they had only just rebuilt her.

Less than a year earlier, fishermen poured milk in the bilges of the newly refurbished *Serigne Mansor*, a sixty-three-foot purse seiner flagged to Mbour. They painted the inside of her hull turquoise to ward off evil spirits. Inside her bow they wrote, in white, the letter *waw*. Her tall young captain, Ousou Boye, had a successful run hauling herring and mackerel.

Every full-moon week a gale rises off the coast of Joal and sends forth a quick succession of uncommonly high waves. Last night such moonchurned waves ripped the anchor line of the *Serigne Mansor*, flipped her onto the beach half a mile south of the *Sakhari Soiré*, then stirred her broken carapace round and round until her stern, transom pointing inland, lay two dozen paces away from the bow; until sand and brown seaweed buried most of the black and green nylon mile of her pursenet, and the splintered midship that had borne the first part of her name, *Serigne*, had washed away into the Atlantic. Like what happened to my boat, says Vieux Sene. Maybe there is consolation in that. From this day on for months her port bow will lie parallel to the tideline so that the turquoise ceiling gapes at Joal, sinking deeper into the sand with each tide.

The *Sakhari Soiré* has only one anchor. Ndongo disregards the implied criticism. Maybe it is a superstitious obligation, a collective way to protect against ruinous envy a precious and expensive vessel that bears the stamp of a famous master shipwright, belongs to a respected elder, and will be piloted by an esteemed fisherman. Or maybe it is, in fact, envy, best left without response. Or maybe water has clogged Ndongo's ears and he is at the moment a little bit deaf. One way or another, he does not react to the kedge talk. In his quiet captain voice he says:

One small leak. It's a nail. I'll fix it tomorrow. I'm happy. Very happy. Great boat. Let's go eat.

We walk to the *mbaar* and squat and sit and stand around a huge tin platter of ceremonial food Fatou Diop Diagne and Ndongo's eldest wife, Alassane, prepared for the launch: *lakh* drowned in sweet yogurt. Amadou sits heavily on a bench made from a mahogany boat keel, removes his sunglasses, folds them into the chest pocket of his boubou.

First, he says, we shall pray. The fishermen and boys around the platter dutifully bow their heads, turn their palms toward heaven. Little Ousseynou, who has been dashing in and out of the sea, is caught by the invitation to prayer with his too-small blue-jeans full of sand and halfway down his wet legs. His face becomes solemn and he tries to wiggle into the tight pants while holding up his hands in prayer. It does not work. He shoots his grandfather a panicked look. Amadou beats his male progeny liberally and often, all of them, even Ndongo. Sometimes the women end up calling the gendarmes. But Amadou has his eyes closed and is talking to God, asking to help his new pirogue to journey in peace, to catch lots of fish, to carry her crew to sea and back safely. He does not see his grandson's predicament. Ousseynou gives up on the pants and prays bare-assed.

▽ ▲ ▽

N dongo skips through the evening harbor. He slaps the bottoms of young fishwives. He steals watermelon slices out of their hands. His wet gym suit still drips seawater. He is on top of the world. He owns the world. Malick and Gora and Vieux walk two steps behind their friend. They are headed to the marina where the pirogues unload their catch because one of their friends' boats just came in from a two-week trip to the Gambia and they are going to ask her crew for some free fish.

After the sun sets the pale-green horizon fades to yellowish blue then to purple. Seabirds rush to their mangrove nests before the longest night of the year swallows the West African coast. The long sedges curve and draw out over the *Sakhari Soiré* and the dwarved *Sakhari Souaré* next to her and the broken *Serigne Mansor* and the blue *Mansor Sakho* and all the other boats. When the birds are gone it is dark and the full moon is right overhead and the beach seems cast of mercury.

That night the *Sakhari Soiré* does not come off her mooring nor does she bilge on her anchor in the waves. The sea holds her up. The sea holds up nothing except itself, holds up everything.

▽ ▲ ▽

I n the waking mangroves by the red road from Fadiouth a murmuration of weavers spools out of the sole acacia tree where they chitter each dawn in the leafless thicket. Long scarves of them billow and contract and billow and contract and stretch, pull in different directions and divide into peripatetic mushroom clouds that flow one into another again, condensing and expanding, pulling, shapeshifting, glorious over a millet-threshing field in the early morning. The loudness of them on the wing over the withered stalks is like an echo of the ocean, upon whose brightening morning chop somewhere now bounces the *Sakhari Soiré*. Her maiden voyage is taking her south to the Gambia and farther on, to Casamance, where fishermen say there are some fish now. Where she will stay for longer than a month. Where, Amadou Souaré has decreed, I am not welcome to come.

Why? He does not say. Maybe he is being protective of his new boat. The *Sakhari Soiré* has her Senegalese papers but she has no permit to fish in Gambian waters. My white skin would attract the attention of the Gambian coastguard. Fishing without a permit would cost the Souarés the motor, the pirogue, maybe even time in Gambian prison.

Or maybe the old man is protective of me. Maybe he is not

convinced that the new pirogue is sturdy enough, though she took two months to build and was launched on the shortest day of the year and blessed at a full-moon tide. The sea is quite cold now, too cold to float to shore alive, the voyage is long.

Yet he is putting aboard every able-bodied man in his bloodline, everyone except for his eldest grandson, Ousmane, whose mother Alassane refuses to let him go on a long trip because she wants the boy to bring home money daily so she can play the lottery. Besides, Ousmane's ailment now has spread from his ulcerous lip to his right eyelid, which has puffed up to the shape and color of an eggplant. A doctor at the town hospital diagnosed it as an allergy and prescribed that Ousmane stop eating sardinella. The diet makes no difference. It is sardinella season; Ousmane handles the fish daily on the pursenetter of Captain Lamine Coura, where he is now an *oupa*. The new captain nags the boy as much as Ndongo did. The badgering, Ousmane says, makes him tired.

Maybe Amadou does not want me aboard because I am a woman. Everyone knows that women aboard are ill-omened. Some fishermen say even crossing paths with a woman before a trip means they will catch no fish. Such men wait for their wives and daughters and mothers and sisters and aunts and female cousins and servant girls to be asleep or at the market or in their rooms before they sneak out to go to sea. They also say a fisherman will have no fish if he has a pregnant wife. Or if he washes with soap.

But I have sailed aboard Amadou's small pirogue many times

already. Besides, Amadou says I can come aboard when the *Sakhari Soiré* sails near Joal—when there are fish here, whenever that may be. So this is not an all-out ban from coming aboard. Perhaps there exists an equation, a time-luck continuum, which permits a woman aboard for eighteen hours but not for several weeks. I cannot know. I have stared at the sea enough to assume that I understand nothing, that I will know only enough to ask: Sailing on which tide?

The *Sakhari Soiré* sails off without me. A magicked barque. Broken by a colonial relic then raised from the dead; hauled, pushed, cajoled, cursed at, blessed, launched on the solstice. A resuscitated semiderelict pile of redwood held together by nails and caulk and charms that herself holds all the hope and all the loss in her phoenix hull. That bears my name on her stern, punctures the false and real membranes between the land and the sea, between truth and myth, between the storyteller and the story.

Exiled, grounded, I beg onto other men's pirogues.

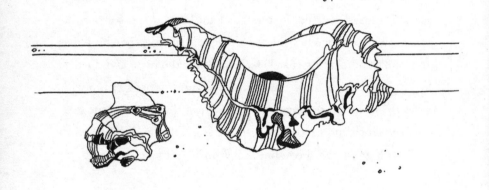

Nine

Winter brings pied avocet and ringed plover, brings curlew sandpiper and red knot and whimbrel. Brings Audouin's gull, one of the world's most rare. Birds come from the Arctic tundra of the Yamal Peninsula and Yakutia, from Mongolia, from Spain. Tens of thousands, hundreds of thousands. Their collective wingbeat charts the course of the annual migratory route of ninety million birds, the East Atlantic Flyway. They have magnetic sensing, like compasses. They know no borders. They follow thermals down coasts.

It happens that when seabirds fly at dawn or sunset, speeding to breakfast or back to roost in perfect unswerving chevrons, they suddenly collapse! collapse for no reason you can see! swerve so chaotically and with such frenetic violence your heart sinks and you think the world is ending—has ended—and then just as suddenly they recover and re-form and continue in their chaste formation, as if nothing has ever happened, as if you didn't just nearly die from heartbreak.

This year the birthdays of Jesus and Muhammad fall on the same week. Mawlid singers quiet and carolers take over beneath the waning supermoon until Mawlid songs start again. This devotional round goes on and on for days, a tidal movement that culminates with Christmas Mass, when the festive bells of Joal's churches clang deep into the chilly night.

By four-thirty on Christmas morning the only music is the forlorn song of dogs howling in the dark, the braying of donkeys, the surf's diaphragmic exhale upon the dark shore. Under a lonesome orange streetlamp outside his sleeping compound Captain Abou Korea, tall and wearing a beige knit sweater with a shawl-collar and a matching wool scarf under his slicker, takes a minute to curse out his no-show crew.

Motherfucker, he says. The hardest thing in fishing is having a crew who don't want to work. I have two young men who work for me. Lead-swingers. Slackers. They live just over there. So I go to wake them up just now and one says he has a stomachache and the other says he has an earache! Why couldn't they tell me this last night?

Now it is just Abou Korea, who is fifty years old, and his son Alassane, who is sixteen. On top of that, the horsecart that usually drives Abou Korea's outboard to the boat does not turn up.

The captain will have to lug the motor to the boat himself. Three blocks of ankle-deep sand, fifty feet of cold, dark water. He is still recovering from back surgery for a cyst.

Sha-ta-ta-ta-ta, he sighs. Oy oy oy. Motherfucker.

He hoists the motor on his shoulder, spits, swears once more, and walks through the black toward the invisible shore. Alassane and I carry drinking water, fuel, the bowlight, the tool bucket, a bailing can, a bucket with a teapot and shotglasses and coal, burden boards, spare net. It takes us three runs. Alassane makes one extra, to the bakery, returns cradling to his chest four fragrant hot baguettes wrapped in newspaper: Oslo's *Aftenposten* and Dakar's *Le Soleil* from two weeks back. In dark alleys things slink as we pass. Dog shadows. Maybe ghosts. In overcast night I guess the tideline inaccurately, step by accident into frigid surf, hypothesize Abou Korea's stooping presence. He taps my arm.

Can you haul net?

Sure. I brought my gloves.

You're my crew today, then.

▽ ▲ ▽

The *Le Fut Budos*, thirty feet, fifteen horsepower, is painted the red, blue, and white of the French tricolor. Abou says the pirogue is named after a town in Gascony because a Frenchman from there gave him the money to build her. Manned with half her normal crew and at half throttle to conserve fuel, she sets sail to west-southwest shortly after five A.M. with her red bowlight blinking. Stirs soft contrails of luminescence as she eases away from shore. Alassane secures buckets and cans neatly in their proper holds, arranges burden boards into a platform amidships, climbs onto it, folds his legs under him very carefully, and falls instantly asleep. It will take hours to get there at this pace.

Away from the mottled darkness of Joal the sea is mostly calm and gray, gray sky, stars and moon almost completely behind cloud. The east begins to pale at six-forty and Venus is swollen above a fogbank touched with the palest blues of predawn. Abou Korea sets before him a square wooden box and opens the lid. Inside is a large compass with a fluorescent ring around the face.

On cloudless nights Abou Korea navigates by the stars; during the day by the position of the sun, the direction of the waves, but it is not day yet and the stars are cast over. He has GPS, too, but does not want to run down the battery. He consults the compass every few minutes and launches into a recitation of all the things that are wrong with the sea nowadays, his personal variation of every fisherman's refrain. Big pursenetters go too fast, very dangerous for smaller boats. Marine sanctuary officials are corrupt. The government takes the fishermen's taxes and duties but offers no social security in return. There are too many boats and too little fish. And what about all the mollusk flags where we are going? So many flags, sha-ta-ta-ta-ta.

Not talking to me nor to his sleeping son but simply to keep himself awake. A trick of the trade.

▽ ⚎ ▽

The highlights of luminescence are gone and water just slips past now. Altocumulus billows lay stepladders across the sky, imitate ocean swells. At seven A.M. the east is dusty orange, Venus bright but fading in layered silkscreen sky, and insects onboard wake up: a white moth, a disoriented wasp, accidental voyagers. Seagulls arrive, singly. The tide is going out and the flags we pass tilt to westward. Some mollusk boats appear, fade out.

Abou Korea fishes his GPS out of his slicker pocket, checks the direction. Four miles to go. He shuts it down again. He has not checked the nets since before the full moon.

Let's see what kind of fish I got.

Fish, in Abou Korea's parlance, are murex, cymbium— anything in the sea. A common tenderness. Fishermen also do not say that fish or mollusk spawn; they say they give birth. But at the harbor all fishers call their catch "product."

I want to finish the job by three in the afternoon. It will be hard shorthanded. Because my crew are shits. Oy-oy-oy-oy. Alassane, though, he is reliable. He will do what I say. Alassane! Alassane! Eh! Psst! Wake up! We're almost there.

The boy sits up, then stands, pulls on a yellow slicker and green slicker pants that have lost their suspenders long ago. He ties them on with a length of green fishline. The sea runs blood orange in all directions.

▽ ▲ ▽

A murex net is about five hundred feet long, a little over a foot wide. Plastic bottles poured full of concrete anchor its ends to the ocean floor, stretch it wide. From each anchor runs a line to a buoyed flag. Abou Korea's flags are made of orange mesh onion bags and black strips of tarp. Today the *Le Fut Budos* must haul and check and pick seventeen nets, then set them again. But the first net she hauls belongs not to Abou Korea but to a fisherman from Djifer. Four days ago Abou Korea watched this man set net too close to his. He tried to warn him away but the man would not listen, probably thought that Abou Korea wanted more murex to himself. Now, the full moon waves of the last week have tangled and twisted the two nets into a shaggy benthic mess fastened tight by hundreds of mollusk clasps.

There are crimpled scallops and cymbium and crabs, and there are minuscule clams that stick to clusters of brown seaweed, and there is red seaweed, frilled and hard and slightly bitter to the taste, and there are tiny florets of pink and yellow and white marine flowers. There are amorphous blobs of man-o-wars that unfold exquisitely the second you toss them back in the sea, each medusa dancing its own singular pulse. There are sharp small barnacles and large beaked triangles of Chautard's pen shell that look like broken-off pike heads and that sometimes bear black pearls, which no fisherman here sees because you toss these shells

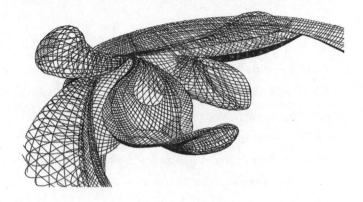

right back into the sea. You don't eat them. Maybe somewhere else in the world, but not here. The snarled nets are heavy with shells and rattle like maracas.

Motherfucker, grumbles Abou Korea. I've been a fisherman for almost forty years. And tell you what: the profession is destroyed. By lack of discipline and by greed.

The more the captain talks, the more worked up he becomes.

Sha-ta-ta-ta-ta-ta. At the *mbaar*, drinking tea and talking, they all look like men. But you know a real worker when you go to sea.

We spend the next four hours picking, untwining, tearing. No one sings. The snarl seems interminable. Around ten-thirty the wind picks up, the sequined sea ripples, tosses the unanchored boat on glittering high tide chop. By one o'clock the wind dies and in its place come flies, lethargic and clingy. From where do they appear suddenly in the afternoon, fifteen nautical miles off-shore? Abou Korea complains:

The amount of years I have spent on the sea? I pray that Alassane doesn't spend them in the sea. Just want him to do anything else, really, that is not in the sea. The problem in this area is that away from the sea there aren't any jobs that pay.

The ocean in late afternoon is slow green molasses that slides under the boat. Not much murex today. Abou Korea blames the wind: in big waves the mollusk burrows into the sea floor to avoid being tumbled. By the time the sun sets we will have picked four nets out of seventeen, with a box of murex to show for it. It will sell for exactly the price of a tank of fuel.

Motherfucker, Abou Korea says. I don't think I've ever been this tired. Sha-ta-ta-ta-ta-ta! May we never know such exhaustion in the afterlife. Alassane, I think maybe we should take out the murex nets and switch to cymbium nets instead.

Okay, Dad.

I pull shake smack grab pry. Under my wet, awkward fingers sea creatures stick pale protuberances out of triangular white shells with narrow orange-yellow trim. I yank at lines and tug them free and pin their pleats down to the bilges with my foot. Sand and shell fragments and seaweed spray and lodge in my hair and eyebrows, weigh down my eyelashes, gristle inside my mouth. My pen and soggy notepad are stashed away somewhere. I am a deckie. I sprain my thumb.

That afternoon a dragonfly latches onto the seat of Alassane's rubberized pants and hitchhikes on his ass all the way to shore.

▽ ▲ ▽

A month later, full-moon waves drag Abou Korea's shadefish trammel onto the rotten skeleton of a pirogue that capsized off Sangomar thirty-five years earlier. The net snags. Sha-ta-ta-ta-ta. It's an expensive net. Abou Korea anchors the *Le Fut Budos* to the net and revs the fifteen-horsepower motor high and the trammel rips, and rips again when Abou Korea tries to hook it off the shipwreck from a different angle. After that, the net would not budge at all. Sha-ta-ta-ta-ta. God protect us against Satan. Motherfucker. The captain grinds his motor, breaks off a piece of his own pirogue's bowsprit. Two hours later he lets it go at last, promises to return—then runs out of fuel within swimming distance of Djifer and has to flag down a passing pirogue to siphon off some gasoil. He spent six miles worth of fuel trying to haul the goddamned trammel. When he returns for it two weeks later the net is gone.

I run into Abou Korea one afternoon near Mbaar Sarrené, where he is mending cymbium net. He beckons me, then lies down on his bad back on the beach sand next to the *mbaar* and from there looks me in the eye and tells me that his fishermen friends blame me for the lost net, say that bringing a woman aboard his pirogue caused this bad luck.

Abou Korea makes lying on the sand seem dignified. I stand next to him, awkward and small.

Do you think it was because of me, Captain?

Ah. I don't know. Probably not. Fishermen are superstitious.

His eyes let go of my face then and he turns his head to look past me at the pale-blue sea. Then he says:

The next day I caught four shadefish with another net, more than a hundred and fifty dollars at the harbor.

Abou Korea does not remember the name of the sunken boat, but knows her captain, Mamadou Ndiaye, who survived the capsize with the crew.y

▽ ▲ ▽

About thirty miles south of here, at the depth of fifty-nine feet, lie the remnants of the MV *Le Joola*, a Senegalese ferry that capsized in a storm off the Gambia in 2002 with nearly two thousand passengers onboard. The sinking ship deployed a single lifeboat. The government of Senegal turned down international offers of assistance and did not dispatch rescue teams for hours. Most of *Le Joola*'s sixty-four survivors were plucked out of the sea by fishermen.

▽ ▲ ▽

Under the eucalyptus tree between the hospital and Mbaar Sarrené the fishermen have switched from belote to checkers. Their checkerboards are sheets of plywood graphed with magic markers, their checkers are yellow and red soda caps, their benches are pirogue boards propped up on cinderblocks. Before lunchtime their little square fills with kitchen smells: boiling rice, boiling fish, pepper sauce, monosodium glutamate.

From their shaded vantage they can watch the winter days blow out to sea in a procession of pirogues: first mollusk boats then gillnetters then pursenetters if the moon is not full. In a full moon gillnetters stay put because moonlight overpowers the luminescence churned up by fish schools and you cannot see the fish. They can watch the comings and goings of neighbors: Christian children in plastic domino masks for Mardi Gras; Gambia and his friends tired from overnight trips to ghostliness; Serer boys bareback on chestnut horses at full gallop on the evening beach; teenage girls playing football outside Abou Korea's house, skirts hiked up to their thighs; Marie Badiane, the mother of the drowned fisherman Action. She has not been to the harbor since her son died.

How do you make a living now, Marie?

Oh, you know, this and that. It's just hard to see the port yet, all the boats coming in. But soon, soon, inshallah. All our hope is in the sea.

Along the beach to the south of the gamblers wind and waves have flattened half the burial mounds. If that was what they were. Ripe Sodom's apples tremble over the dunes.

▽ ▲ ▽

K nowledge, Captain Daouda Sarr tells me, is doing things.
But the more things I do, the more everything I thought I
knew seems to flatwash into a watery vagueness, amorphous and
changeable, where all definitions are recharted and relearned, all
lines crossed, all meanings slippery. I helped build a pirogue—
and so what of it? She is plying some distant seas unknowable to
me. And I? Again it comes, this familiar and implaceable lostness,
this sense of dislocation that feels as if I am overlooking something important yet ineffable, missing something I cannot quite
identify. It feels, too, queerly shameful, the way it rises from the
gut as a deep blush, a gasp: what have I done? My mother once
described hot flashes this way.

Now I am bailing the *Stacko Mbacké*, Daouda's thirty-foot gillnetter. Her crew are Daouda's uncle Gorgui Sarr, who is fifty-nine
years old and has spent half of his life in Spain, and Daouda's
nephew Babou Sarr, twenty-four and very large and gawky, as if
his body's boundaries are yet unknown to him, as if he is still
growing. When Babou walks on gunwales the wood creaks.

Don't break my boat, eh!

To me, Daouda continues to speak in riddles, in koans. Are
gris-gris powerful because of the magic locked within them or
because of the magic they represent? Does medicine heal because
of its chemical properties or because you believe it will work?
Presently he asks:

How long will it take you to learn to bail?

What do you mean?

To bail! To bail! Me, I am still learning to bail. I have been a captain for thirty years and I am still learning to fish. What can you teach me?

What indeed. What the sea teaches best: to gorge—to gorge on beauty. "Every object, well contemplated, awakens a new organ within us," wrote Goethe. A kind of opening that allows for a recognition of the ineffable, guides through liminal spaces. Look. Low orange sun illuminates the black smog from the Tann Ba smokers that masses over the receding skyline of Joal. Large pink man-o-wars float past the pirogue, and upon the placid surface of late afternoon sea the wake of small murex boats returning to shore is a crisscross of spiderweb silk, the thinnest-spun gold thread. In the white sky a duck flies. Then ten more ducks; they bank and pick up at once and bank again.

Seasonal birds, like more than two hundred other species on this coast, most of them Palearctic. Fewer come each year. Cities and deserts swallow their habitats, men hunt their kin, pesticides poison their eggs. Climate change uncouples the timing of resource from the timing of migrations, syncopates their traveling cycles, puts the birds out of step with themselves. The birds are confused.

What if all birds the world over moved somehow in synchronicity imperceptible to humans? All the birds everywhere on the planet tied by a perfect and omnipresent choreography of which only we flightless mammals were oblivious? I don't know about that, Daouda says. I know that fish are like birds. They lay eggs in Europe but every year they return here at the same time. And their children do as well. Fish do the same.

On the *Stacko Mbacké* men pray for fish. Gorgui bends low, touches forehead to gunwale. Daouda, left hand on the throttle, mouths a prayer, touches his solar plexus with his right. Then he begins to sing in a full open tenor, in Arabic, an ode to Cheikh Amadou Bamba's favorite disciple, the dreadlocked Ibrahima Fall, who promoted hard labor as a form of worship:

Oh, Cheikh Ibrahima Fall!

No one can be as powerful as you.

Give us something no one can take away from us.

Give us light!

Oh, la illaha illa Allah!

Oh, la illaha illa Allah!

The hymn rolls with the ebb tide and the sea is blue and smooth and in its mellow waters the sun quivers like yolk.

∇ ∆ ∇

Eighteen miles offshore. At six-thirty a sudden breeze furrows the chop. Men cast net. They cast in a straight line, as all gillnetters do at night, stretch its hanging panel in the middle of the sea: this is called a driftnet. Daouda cuts the engine, anchors the pirogue, comes over to midships, and sits down on the burden boards, the back of his neck against a thwart.

And now, he says, we wait—and we wait—and we wait—

Babou chimes in:

—and we wait—and we wait—

Then Gorgui:

—and we wait—and we wait—

The men are laughing now. They make tea. They pass around bananas. They check net every couple of hours and pick some of the fish out of it and grill it on the boat brazier for supper. Sunset blushes whitecaps pink, golden, red. Northeast wind blows a swarm of bees onto the boat. Daouda watches them with concern. They will not be able to return to shore, he says. They will fly and get tired and land on the water and get wet and never get up again. He is sorrowful for the bees.

Several years ago Daouda Sarr got paid to smuggle a hundred and twenty-one people to Spain aboard an eighty-two-foot pirogue from the tropical forests of Casamance. The boat never made it: she ran out of fuel two-thirds of the way up and drifted until a Moroccan coastguard cutter towed her to shore. All aboard ended up spending nearly two months in a Moroccan prison. Long enough that Daouda learned to speak Arabic. When smugglers offered to hire him again, he refused. What I was hoping for in Spain was to eat until my belly was full and to live in peace, he says. And all of that I have here now.

The sun melts into a triangle, a pyramid, a square, a pink stripe. Last seabirds in silhouette. Nothing.

Split neatly in two perfect halves the moon rocks directly overhead, directly below the bowsprit. Daouda waits until it sets in a flaxen stripe, then steers slowly alongside the net so we can haul it in segments. In black sea the yellow row of buoys is a lubber's line. We begin to pick. Large sardinella, slippery with winter oil; those were the first fish ever canned, two hundred years ago, to feed Napoleon's army. Mackerel with razor gills. Halfbeaks with startlingly soft bellies. Flat bonga shad. In moonlessness the sea worries, the waves rise, angry chop grows. Bioluminescence trickles down my water-wrinkled fingertips, lights up my toes when I wiggle them in cold bilgewater, bubbles into the boat with the leaks: myriads of protozoa smacking against one another, against the inwales, the thwarts, the fish. Soon I am too tired to notice. I pick and bail and pick with unbending fingers and bail again. Around four in the morning, barely awake and numb from the cold, we head back to port.

Oh, Cheikh Ibrahima Fall,

You are the light!

Oh, la illaha illa Allah,

You are a strong man!

Oh, la illaha illa Allah!

Oh, la illaha illa Allah!

Daouda sings. Mollusk flags pop at us out of the darkness: eerie cemeteries of flags. We reach Joal by six and anchor just offshore. There are some pirogues. The shore is empty yet, dark, no one to buy our fish. Babou snores loudly in the bow. The rest of us bob in and out of sleep. Our limbs are leaden from fatigue and cold. Gorgui lights the brazier to make a pot of hot sweet tea and other brazier lights flicker on other boats in the sleepy marina

where other frozen fishermen, exhausted to the threshold of delir-
ium, wait on their anchored boats to find out their catch's worth.

The *Stacko Mbacké* unloads her fish at dawn. Daouda's two
wives, Fatou and Seynabou, stand together on the shore, petite,
pretty, warm. One of Seynabou's legs is slightly shorter than the
other, a memento from when she was a little girl and a vaccination
she got at Joal's hospital became infected and the doctors ended
up cutting out the festering chunk. The women wave. They smile.
During the six months of the day-fishing season Daouda spends
two nights in a row with one wife, then switches. But when he
comes home from night fishing he goes to bed with the one who
puts his laundry in the washtub first, even if it is the same wife
every morning. Which wife will keep him warm today? I do not
want to guess.

I stumble home on woozy legs. Men hired a tractor to drag off
the beach the stern of the *Serigne Mansor*, the gillnetter that shipwrecked on winter solstice, but her bow remains a dark crag rising from the night sand, mostly buried under the washings of
weeks of high tides, irretrievable. Her net forever lost. On the
dark beach near the smashed boat a teenage boy in wet briefs, all
ashy goosebumps and sinew, has moored his father's pirogue to a
palmtree stump and now is trying to find his pant leg with a
sandy foot.

Psst, white woman! Eh! You went fishing?

Yes.

La illaha illa Allah! Today?

Yes.

And after you sold the fish at the harbor, did you get your share?

Of course. I always get my share.

▽ ▲ ▽

M y landlords are still asleep when I come home. I unlock the compound gate and heat up a bucket of water on a propane burner. My bath sponge is recycled from blue and green gillnet; fishermen in Mbaar Sarrené make sponges like this. I put my laundry in a plastic washtub, sprinkle it with detergent. I will get to it later. I fall asleep in sweaty morning by myself.

▽ ▲ ▽

N ight-fishing season in full swing. For weeks I go to sea for twenty hours at a time and pick net in moonlight. On departing pirogues my crewmates call their girlfriends until there is no more cellphone signal and no more daylight and from then on each boat charts a shimmering course through bioluminescent sea in majestic isolation. Fish schools whirl underwater in sparkler circles. I take bucket showers afterward but still find fish scales on my pillow after morning naps. I dream I am growing gills.

Ashore Joal empties of men. They are either asleep or at sea. Some, like Ndongo, are gone for weeks.

On the way home from the harbor drowsy fishermen ooze into Mariama Boye's breakfast shack.

Salaam aleikum, Mariama, how are things?

Al ham du lillah—we're still alive.

Where is Gora?

He's fishing in the Gambia.

Eh! Your husband, Gora, is going to take a second wife.

That's right, he'll take a Gambian wife!

Yes, he'll take a Gambian wife and she will cook him nice dinners.

She will wash his clothes and bathe him!

And she will spend nights with him!

Many men marry in the Gambia, like my neighbor Mariama Thiam's husband, who never returned. I know one pursenetter captain who married his third wife in the Gambia. Now he has one wife in Joal, one in Mbour, one in the Gambia.

You got a woman in every port!

That's right. This way if I am fishing and I go to Mbour, I always have a dinner and a bed, or if I go to Joal or to the Gambia, I always have a dinner and a bed, too. This is what I call a man!

He adds:

I'd also like to have a wife in England.

Why, you plan to go fishing in England?

Why not?

Mariama Boye smiles at the fishermen's taunts. Her big arms, big face, long golden earrings that brush her round shoulders, her soothing kindness. She offers refills on the coffee, another boiled egg, some extra mayo on that po'boy. When the men leave she wipes baguette crumbs off the table with a rag, straightens the pots of bean sauce, onion sauce, boiled noodles; makes sure all the lids are on tight. She wipes her hands very slowly. Then she says:

You know? Maybe he will. Maybe he will marry another woman, in the Gambia. He always keeps going to the Gambia.

After Mariama closes shop, Taïf the mechanic begins a busy day. It is late winter. As shadows grow shorter, queues at repair shops grow longer: pirogues have to travel so far to catch anything these days that all the outboard motors are acting up.

It could also be the dirt, Abou Korea says. Aboard the *Le Fut Budos* we pick nets that are soiled brownblack, greasy. What is it? He does not know. Maybe crude oil. I bring the net to my face, smell it, but the mesh, like everything, smells of fish and seabrine. This kind of dirt often comes this time of the year, but it will pass, Abou Korea says. The ocean current circles around, sometimes it brings dirt, sometimes fish, sometimes nothing. The sea is so.

Every few days the women of the Souaré household relay the latest bearings for the *Sakhari Soiré*. Now she is in the Gambia. Now she is in Casamance. Now Ousmane has hitched a ride south with another pirogue and joined the crew. With most men out of the house, Fatou Diop Diagne sets up a breakfast stand inside her compound. At five o'clock every morning she drags a large wooden desk under an awning of corrugated tin, sends a grandchild out to the bakery for a heap of baguettes, heats up last night's oily onion yassa sauce, murex sauce, pea sauce, spaghetti, and sits down facing the gate with her embroidery in her lap to wait for customers.

For a few years after Fatou moved to Joal with her young husband, she made quite a bit of money braiding women's hair at the harbor, which was farther south then, down the alley from my room. But one day Amadou told her to stop. He said she braided hair very well for strangers instead of cooking very well for the house. After that Fatou no longer braided hair for money.

For the next twenty-five years she would walk to the harbor, ask her husband's fishermen buddies for free fish, and sell the fish in the market at a twofold markup. That was when she and Amadou build this big house: poured concrete patio floor, tiles in every room and under the awning, blue walls, blue and red metal window shutters, an indoor shower, and a flush toilet. Back then, if you made thirty dollars a day by reselling fish it felt as if you had made no money at all. Now you can't expect to make ten. Now Fatou buys shrimp in Joal and resells it in Dakar during the shrimping season, but even then there are often too few shrimp to make the trips worthwhile.

It used to be, too, that the pirogue's daily share of earnings covered the cost of all three meals for everyone in the house. But a few years ago Fatou had to change the rules: two hot meals a day on the house, everyone buys their own breakfast. Now they can buy it from her. But today the crew are gone and it seems no one in the neighborhood is hungry. Her breakfast stall is neglected, her wares untouched. Fatou fans herself in a plastic chair beneath a clothesline draped with little boys' gym clothes and translucent women's panties, and chants:

Where, oh where, are the people who will buy my food? Selling breakfast doesn't work today. Sha-ta-ta-ta-ta, it doesn't work.

It's because the sea hasn't been working this year, says Amadou. It's the second month of night-fishing season and we are all still waiting for fish. No one has enough money for your po'boys.

Fatou nods. A mouse runs between her blue chair and the blue wall, scurries past the tulle door curtain into Alassane's bedroom. There, a large laminated photograph of the *Sakhari Soiré* floats over a painted backdrop of an orange sunset, blue clouds, blue surf, and a volcano such as studded this coast once, helped form it millions of years back. The picture, taken from the starboard side of the boat, occupies the prime spot of the three-tiered iconostasis of faded pink photographs of Sufi cheikhs and women made up beyond recognition. Alassane put it in the center of the very top row, under a large brown teddybear, next to a photoshopped collage of caliphs and marabouts of the smallest of Senegal's four Sufi brotherhoods, the Layenne.

The Layenne say that after the death of the Prophet, the Light of Muhammad—which God had created long before anything else, before heaven and Earth, before the oceans and the empyrean, and which emanated from the finger of Adam and from the forehead of his wife Hawwa—resided in a volcanic blowhole on the Atlantic shore of Dakar. In French the Layenne call it *la Sainte Grotte de la Lumière*: the Sacred Cavern of Light; in Wolof they call it *Xûnt-mi*: the Cave.

From there for more than a thousand years the Light of Muhammad emerged nightly on a divine search. At last, in the middle of the nineteenth century, it found what it had been looking for: Libasse Thiaw, a hereditary Lebou fisherman from Dakar. When he turned forty—a mystical number that signifies rebirth and renewal; the amount of years it took Mousa to walk Jews out of Egypt; the age of Muhammad when Archangel Jibril revealed to him that he was the God's messenger—Thiaw proclaimed himself Seydina Mouhammadou Limamou Laye, the Prophet incarnate.

Like the Prophet, Limamou Laye was illiterate, cast no shadow, and left no footprints on sand, though you could see his tracks on hard rock. There is one still by the Cave—you can touch it. He sermonized in Wolof, preached austerity, healed the sick, exorcized the possessed, and prophesied his own imprisonment by the French, which lasted three months. Like the Prophet, Limamou Laye was initially pronounced mad. Eventually he gained a following and established the Layenne brotherhood. He outlived the Prophet and died in 1909, at the age of sixty-six.

They say the Light of Muhammad still lingers in *Xûnt-mi*. The cave is in a compound not far from the pale fortress of the United States embassy, almost to the westernmost point of continental Africa. A stuccoed wall delimits the compound. No one guards its two gates. Signs on the wall declare it a holy site and caution visitors to dress modestly. You pass a custodian's house where goats chew on garbage and laundry ripples on the line, you pass a large gazebo where pilgrims from far away take their rest. The

Atlantic is rough here, always in whitecaps. You leave your shoes on the concrete steps that lead toward the edge of a cliff jutting into the sea. The steps end in a small patch of sand. The custodian always keeps the sand freshly raked to erase any visitor's tracks, like the Prophet's. To your left, if you face the ocean, a hole. An aluminum ladder squeezes vertically down into the narrow dark. You descend past the sea-tortured crenellations of brownblack rock into a deep womb where suddenly two openings of light whirl out to westward: the cave's two proximate mouths, lit up a pale blue by the sea. You stand in the warm surf, you remember: in the beginning, or soon thereafter, God split the Light of Muhammad in two to create water and heaven.

Pray, says the caretaker. He has slid down the ladder after you. He touches your arm, offers up his palms to the cave's igneous roof, to the sea: pray like this. Now put your head here. A tiny shoulder-level grotto, fragrant. Does it smell of the incense the custodian rubs into it day after day or of the perfume thousands of pilgrims brought here on their hair, faces, necks? They say Muhammad always smelled of camphor and civet musk, that he never rejected a gift of perfume.

Pray again, the custodian says, then go up. He is so fast, why is he in such a hurry? A blast of wet wind picks up your skirt. Up in the sun you blink to see what you missed before your descent: an irregular indentation in a chunk of basalt. The imprint of Limamou Laye's foot. Now put your right foot into his imprint. See how much bigger his foot was than yours? Now rest your left knee here, in this indentation. Pray. Pray.

All efforts to fix on photographic plate the image of Limamou Laye have produced nothing but blankness. But there exists an image of his son, who was born with a birthmark that spelled on his chest, in Arabic, the name Issa: Jesus. The Layenne confirmed Seydina Issa Rohou Laye as the reincarnation of Jesus when he was thirty-three years old; after his father's death he became the first caliph of the Layenne. In his portrait you can make out the Greek letters alpha and omega in the folds of his turban. This stenciled image now watches over Dakar from many walls— including the wall of the *Xûnt-mi* compound. On this particular portrait, on the turban, someone has written in big block letters: BABY.

▽ ▲ ▽

The Layenne celebrate Christmas and believe a pilgrimage to Mecca unnecessary. When they ablute before each of the five daily prayers they wash their legs all the way up to their knees. Almost all Layenne are Lebou fisherfolk. Fatou Diop Diagne, Ndongo's mother, is Layenne.

The Lebou number fewer than a hundred thousand people and live almost entirely in Dakar, mostly in Yoff, a tiny semiautonomous fishing theocracy chinked out of a stretch of volcanic beach in the capital's northwest, an hour or so on foot from *Xûnt-mi*. They speak Lebou Wolof, a dialect that has its own names for most fish. Some say the Lebou are a Wolof subgroup, others that they are an ethnic group of their own. Their origins are disputed.

Some say their ancestors fished their way westward from the Red Sea and the Mediterranean, establishing themselves first in Libya around the vanished Lake Tritonis, which Herodotus described as a "great lagoon," before continuing toward the Atlantic and down the coast of Mauritania until they stopped at Cap-Vert peninsula, where Dakar is today. Others say they descended from a band of riparian hunters who trace their origins to Egyptian pharaohs. Fatou Diop Diagne says the Lebou are the same as the Wolof, just more stubborn and a little more difficult to be around.

❦ ⁂ ❦

Millions of dragonflies hatch, speckle the evening sky like television screen static. Tiny asymmetrical stars of horseradish tree flowers get caught in hair and clothes, their heady saccharine fragrance mixes oddly with the smell of fresh and smoked fish and refuse. In the morning, dew begins to gather on beached pirogue gunwales and thwarts, on *mbaar* benches. Somewhere beyond, clouds form and float across the sea, brittle archipelagos of shade.

▼ ▲ ▼

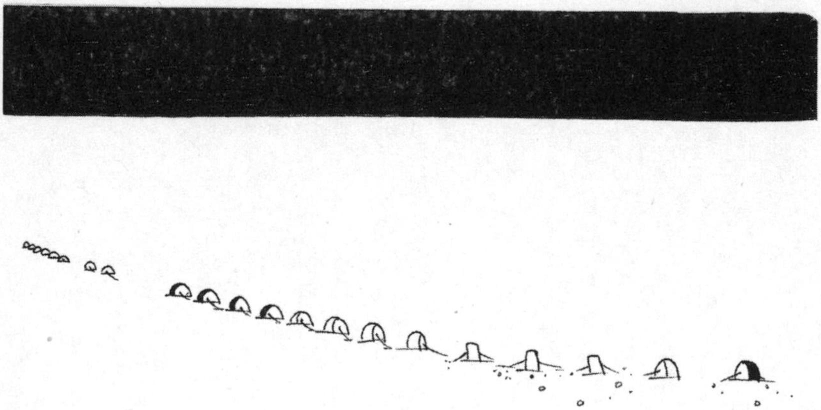

Ten

The ocean glows at night. The pirogue glides upon her own brilliant wake. Fish schools flicker like sunken treasure. You cast net: the Christmas garland of the floatline lights up the instant it hits water, a floating halo in neverending black. Luminescence weeps into the boat through seams in blinking rivulets. You bail buckets of radiance. The outboard motor churns pure light.

When you haul a full net on a moonless night with frigid wet fingers you pull against a coruscating mass of cold fire scooped into the mesh out of the surrounding darkness. Straining against this dazzling hallucination the pirogue rotates under the Milky Way as if on a turntable: so perfectly flat and depthless the sparkling sea, so perfectly flat and depthless the sparkling sky. Fish jump to escape the net, trail the same white blaze as the shooting stars above. Lights of other pirogues tinsel the horizon.

You tip the seine into the boat: Look! Your cuti-
cles twinkle. Fish thrash, spray the thwarts with
glitter, spill light into the holds, each scintillation a
blazing pinprick that lasts a tenth of a second. Soon
the boat is dark again.

∇ ∴ ∇

We were fishing off the Gambia first. Then we were fishing off
Djifer. There were no fish. From what I heard at the harbor there
were more fish here.

But you know how fishermen are. We hear there are fish somewhere, we go there—but fish move.

Yes, they don't wait for us.

After several weeks of lean pickings down south, the *Sakhari
Soiré* is back in Joal. Her crew, bloodshot-eyed, ashy, thin, drape
over chairs and stools in the Souaré courtyard; above them their
torn and faded laundry flaps from clotheslines in midwinter wind
like pennants on a dressing line. Only young Vieux, who has
grown man's muscles on his little boy's frame and has adorned his
wrists with multicolored silicone bands that say ADIDAS, PLAY-
BOY, CHELSEA, mementos of all his ports of call where wristbands
are ten for a buck, seems to have any energy left. He parades his
new jewelry and his new ripped body around the courtyard. He
picks up toddling siblings and halfsiblings, brags to young
Maguette about his marine exploits. His brother Ousmane, face
scaly, skin ashen, stretches out on the floor of his mother's

bedroom—one eye on a French football game on TV, the other swollen shut—and endures Fatou's fuss over his eczemaed face.

Ousmane, how was the Gambia?

Eh! To be honest, it sucked.

Why?

There was no fish.

Did you make any new friends down there?

Some.

Outside a small child screams: someone is pulling a guinea worm out of her leg. Ndongo sails into the room with baby Moustapha, his and Sokhna's youngest, in the crook of his arm, lets him sip water from his tin cup, lets him drool over his stained football jersey, coos. Such a big boy! Look at how much you've grown! Sokhna comes in after them, takes the baby away, laughs.

I have to watch it with Ndongo, she says. He's a fisherman, you know. If I leave Moustapha with him long enough, next thing you know he'll take the baby fishing!

The *Sakhari Soiré* will sail again tomorrow. She will go back to the Gambia, or Casamance, or Sangomar. Wherever there are fish.

The day I am finally allowed to go to sea aboard the new pirogue her captain is Maguette. Ndongo stays ashore. He has hired himself out to mend a friend's seine so he can begin saving the money for his dream: a boat of his own, a purse seiner. Together with a motor and a net the pirogue will cost thirty thousand dollars.

The departure is scheduled for noon, at low tide. Adamantine sky, hard as flint. The pirogue points landward, stretches the hawser tied to her bollard of the day, a keel stub poking out of the sand like a rotten tooth.

For a few minutes before coming aboard Maguette and his crew stand at the tideline and watch the sea. Size it up the way laamb wrestlers size up each other in a ring. Divine it for fish or perhaps treachery. Then Maguette says:

Wallahi, I really would rather fish during the day. Night fishing is exhausting.

Yeah, I hate fishing at night, says El Hadj Ndour. El Hadj is a new hire, a former laamb wrestler who prefers to fish on pursenetters. He is thirty years old. All of his usual boats are away on long trips, so he has hired himself out for the night to the *Sakhari Soiré*.

Six months of this is a lot. In my opinion it should be only three months.

During the day-fishing season, by the time we cast net today I'd already be home, daydreams Maguette. I'd be taking a bath, and my wife would be putting incense in the room, preparing a nice dinner for me.

But this time of the year there's no fish during the day, says Maguette's friend Ibrahima Kama. He is in his early twenties and he, too, has hired himself aboard for the trip because his regular pirogue is having a lay day.

So we must fish at night. But you're right, I hate it, too.

Used to be that in this area there was a lot of bonga shad, says El Hadj. Used to be they would come at the net at such speed they'd rip the net. Wallahi, there used to be a lot of bonga shad here.

The bonga shad catch has decreased by two-thirds in a decade.

Yes, there would be times there'd be so much fish you wouldn't fit it all in the boat, says Cheikh Bathily, Maguette's second mate. You'd call other boats to come pick your net—or you'd mark the spot on a GPS, take what you could carry to sell at the harbor, and then return to pick the rest.

I know! Last year this happened to Coura Kane's brother. They called us to help them pick net. Also Boubacar, the one who lives in the same house as Khady, Ndongo's third wife—happened to him, too.

You can't see any real fish bubbles during the day this time of year anymore, says Cheikh. When I was young you would see a lot of bubbles even during the dry season.

Cheikh is forty and older than any man onboard except for the first mate, Pa Modou Diouf. Pa Diouf used to be Amadou Souaré's first mate back when Amadou still went to sea. He is fifty-six years old, tiny in stature. His only wife and six children grow peanuts and millet on a farm inland that he visits on holidays; the journey is two hours by shared taxi and another half hour by horsecart. Most of the year he lives with the Souarés, in their big house. He was in his twenties when he saw the sea for the first time. The sea was so beautiful, he told me once. It wanted me to stay, so I did.

Pa Diouf does not join the conversation. He rarely does. After a lifetime of chasing mute fish on loud motorboats he mostly whistles and gestures. Talking, he begins—then gives up, waves with both hands, looks away: nuff said. At the Souaré compound he likes to sit in a metal chair out of the sun and nod at the small children who play at his feet.

Men count down to noon. A foot or so above the wrackline a small eddy throbs over a clamshell: a clavicle of ebb tide. The ocean's heartbeat, the first. Maybe the one reliable timepiece in the whole world.

At last Maguette says, *Bismillah*, and the men roll up their sweatpants and tiptoe toward the pirogue, curl the balls of their feet against iceblue winter water like herons. The air is in the upper nineties during the day but the sea is still frigid. Between the boat and the shore a silver school of fry skims the water and momentarily it is as if the sea is turned inside out, exposing some sacred vital organ.

∇ ∆ ∇

The pirogue hugs the shore, points south-southwest. Ousmane is at the helm. Next to him perches Ndiaga Kane, an *oupa* Ousmane's age. In the hold just fore of the helm everyone's flipflops and provisions bags, two car tires for lifesavers, two spare fuel cans, two jerrycans with water. In the next hold, between the sixth and seventh thwarts, Pa Diouf has fallen asleep on a burden board, his head on his green rucksack with a broken zipper. El Hadj sits on the fifth thwart, over the net hold where Maguette has stretched out on the net to make some phone calls; the net around him rises like green spume. Little Vieux, in a small pink hoodie, settles in the bow and cuts up some rotten fish from yesterday's catch for bait. Next to him Cheikh Bathily ablutes with drinking water, prays, then brews strong minty tea. The faded green and blue Arabic calligraphy of prayers inside the boat's ceiling is already illegible, eaten away by saltwater after two months at sea. Fish scales laminate port risers and gunwales.

Ousmane steers his grandfather's boat through the white pall of smoke of Tann Ba. If you see the smoke you know there is fish at the harbor, at least some, at least for some. Steers her southward along the filao and Sodom's apple groves that cinch the soil over unmarked fishers' graves. Across the mellow mouth of the Mama Nguedj, where the outboard snags for several minutes on a large sheet of transparent plastic tarp. Past Fadiouth, above which a giant red *sacré cœur* floats atop the postmodern belfry of the Church of Saint François Xavier, named for a missionary who helped Portugal colonize Asia around the same time as other Portuguese missions assisted the enslavement of West Africa. The heart and the church are brand new, rebuilt after a hurricane shattered the nineteenth-century original almost two decades earlier. The islanders proudly tell visitors that all of Fadiouth's residents,

Christians and Muslims alike, pitched in to rebuild the church. Carved into the new church doors below the heart, invisible from the sea, bas-reliefed wooden fishermen trawl a wooden Atlantic with molded wooden seines.

Each year Fadiouth's residents fortify their teetering tabby homes with sand they scoop from the outlying bars that protect the midden from ocean waves. Soon there will be nothing left to stop a swell from taking out to sea the island's church, the nunnery, the mosques, its entire shell skeleton. *Terra firma*: the term is deceptive.

The *Sakhari Soiré* sails past Tindine Island, a small sandbar between Fadiouth and Palmarin where European colonists once made the Serer cultivate cotton. Only hyenas and genii live on Tindine Island now. If you build a house on the island you will go mad. You will have nightmares, or you will be walking and fall all of a sudden. They say it is safe to step ashore and walk around as long as you intend to leave, but no one really does. No one really disembarks on Tindine, only sorcerers. Wild cotton plants snarl island sand.

At last shore falls astern. A freshening steady sou'wester, unusual for the season, blows damp. The turquoise sea sparkles. Light spray to port. To starboard the wake cuts the sun in two: a shining glob like a bead of oil, and, inside the wake, a mosaic whirlpool of golden sparkles.

In midafternoon the rusted navigational buoy of Sangomar clangs into view, warns sailors of the Point of Sangomar, the genii meeting spot. For more than a hundred years coastal erosion has been severing the landbridge that connects the point with the mainland. Occasionally the point splits entirely. European sailors first began to record the periodic rupture in the late nineteenth century. Nine inches. Eleven inches. Three thousand feet. Two and a half miles at one point. The tide scrapes silt and sand off the mainland and deposits them at the island's southern tip. Takes man's land and delivers it to the genii. In the Saloum River Delta inland from Sangomar, the tide disinterred a body from a village cemetery, then laid it out to dry.

And sixty miles offshore, oil companies have begun to mine the vast deposit of oil and gas that lies five hundred fathoms deep. How will the drilling affect the genii? The fishermen?

No problem! says Ndongo. We'll fish around the rigs.

The way they fish around the vanishing fishstocks, the unpredictable weather, the foreign ships, magic, sickness, life.

White streaks of seagull shit dribble down the buoy's red and white stripes. Above it tiny puffs of cumulus hover; below, the dark green sea reflects meringue sky. A black flipflop and a blue chocolate wrapper sail past on watery clouds. Under the buoy and the jetsam and the clouds real and reflected lie hundreds of millions of barrels of petroleum, unseen riches that will keep men coming here even after the fish are gone.

Ousmane cuts the motor.

Vieux reheats the lunch his mother, Alassane, prepared for the crew: an aluminum basin heaped with rice and a spicy sauce of onions, eggplant, bitter tomato, smoked cymbium, cuttlefish, sardine, and meaty white grouper, once abundant but now overfished and threatened. While we eat with our hands—more delicious this way, the fishermen say—the cumuli concentrate into a haze. Part harmattan, part fog frames a jade seascape. It is astonishingly quiet.

After the meal Vieux leans overboard to wash the basin. Ousmane, in the bow, threads a lighted marker buoy onto the gillnet's floatline, makes sure the two anchors on the leadline are secure. Maguette starts the motor. At five minutes to four the sun throws a handful of flags to the southwest.

The *Sakhari Soiré* circles a pearlescent sea.

Prepare to cast.

Cast net.

El Hadj leans against the gunwale and lowers the green net to the green sea with beautiful long motions, releases it into a straight bottom-set line more than a mile long. A hopeline. An assayed boundary between fish and no fish. Then Maguette steers the boat half a cable's length to westward and drops anchor. It is common to leave a bottom-set net alone. It is also common for a boat to return to find her net shredded by a passing industrial trawler. A torn net costs hundreds of dollars to replace, strands a fisherman ashore. At sea, a torn net becomes a ghostnet, an indiscriminate rogue hunter that continues to snag fish and pelagic birds and marine mammals for years. Ecologists call this ghostfishing.

▽ ▲ ▽

The breeze scores the ocean lightly and evenly, as if someone
has pressed a net into the surface and lifted it. The men wait.
They talk about shariah law and marriage and birth control. Is
it okay to use condoms when having sex with one's wives and is it
okay for the wives to go on the pill? The answer to both questions,
the men decide, is yes. Is it okay to have an abortion? Maybe, if
the pregnancy endangers the life of the mother. Is it okay for the
wife to have her tubes tied (the men cannot agree on this, maybe
if she's old or really sick) or for the husband to have a vasectomy
(wallahi, no no no!). They talk about wives: how many, how old,
where to house them. Same house is cheaper, different houses
quieter. They make references to radio talk shows and Friday
sermons and teachings from the Koranic schools they attended
decades ago. They do not involve me in their colloquy, do not look
at me as they talk. Maybe they have forgotten that I am a woman.
Or maybe they do not care for a woman's opinion on such things.
On their shores the fates of women are ultimately up to men. In
the bow Ousmane and Vieux thread baited hooks onto two
lengths of line, wrap the line around their forefingers, and cast.
Whenever something bites—a sardine, a mackerel—their faces
light up in gorgeous smug surprise, as if this were the first time
they ever had caught fish in their life.

When I was the same age as Ousmane, says Cheikh Bathily,

sometimes we would know what kind of fish we'd catch because before we'd go out on a trip the owner of the boat would see a marabout and make sure we'd catch that specific kind of fish— grouper, for example.

There is a boat that two months ago caught two hundred and ninety-five boxes of grouper in the Gambia, says El Hadj. Forty kilometers from Djifer.

I've never seen that much grouper. But once I was on this boat that caught a hundred boxes of rouget.

We once had a hundred and fifty boxes of blue butterfish. It's good, but man does it smell vile!

Stories. They have kept us afloat since time immemorial. True or false, each one is a buoy of faith. Daouda Sarr says that once upon a time people told children stories at night, and that each story had a moral. Children would learn from these stories, and they would forever remember what to strive for, what to avoid. Back then people farmed or fished, lived simply, had less stuff, and needed less than today. They didn't have to have televisions or cellphones. People worked less and during the offseason they would stay at home. They had the energy and the time to tell stories to their children. Now people want, want, want, and they work very hard and all year long, and they come home tired and have no strength or time to tell their children anything, though Daouda does sing to his children and teaches them the names of their ancestors.

Suddenly Maguette jumps up from the midships thwart.

Motherfucker!

A gillnetter flagged to Djifer, the *El H Lamine Thior*, has sailed up while the *Sakhari Soiré*'s crew were chatting. Now she is casting her net into the sea near Maguette's.

What the hell does he think he's doing? Anchors aweigh!

Maguette runs from thwart to gunwale to the sternsheets pushing off the wood so hard the entire boat shudders and rolls and El Hadj grabs the smoldering brazier to keep it from sliding into the hold. Maguette yanks the starter rope, jerks the choke and yanks the rope again, and on a sputtering motor shoots the pirogue full speed ahead, nearly ramming the other boat with the bow.

Eh! You! The place where you are casting net is too close to ours!

The crew on the other boat pause, lift their faces from the luffing net in silence, consider Maguette where he stands in the stern, seesawing and furious in a trucker's hat embroidered with an American flag and a portrait of Che Guevara. The men aboard the *Sakhari Soiré*, too, watch their captain, also say nothing. A young man in brown overalls at the other boat's helm motions for his men to keep casting, shouts back at Maguette:

What do you want us to do, haul it?

You're too close! Didn't you just see us cast here?

So what? You don't own the sea, do you?

What you're doing is unfair!

The other man turns to his crew. Come on guys, keep casting, let's finish up. He revs the motor. The rest of the *El H Lamine Thior*'s net slips into the water and she speeds off. Maguette gives chase. In close pursuit but not fast enough. The other boat's crew stare straight ahead as he strains alongside. The goddamn motor. He yells to his men:

Grab her net!

Cheikh raises his hand.

Leave her net! Don't fight with them, Maguette. We'll have our chance at sea today, inshallah. Peace is better than fighting. Don't fight with them.

Take her net, I said!

Cheikh stands up, steadies himself in the rocking boat, thrusts out his palm toward his captain.

Maguette. Listen, son. Trust me. It does no good to argue. The same thing happened yesterday, with that other pirogue, and in the end you got more fish than them. It's all a question of luck.

That utterance itself a conjuration. A prayer, a magic spell repeated on every pirogue, in each *mbaar*. Daouda Sarr is not quite right: there is a story fishermen tell the children they take aboard, the same story with the same moral they tell themselves daily, to keep going to sea, to keep going. This is it.

Maguette rages on but slows down to half throttle, steers the boat back to her anchoring spot, mutters to himself. His men look away. The exhaustion of the night-fishing season frays everyone's nerves. Two months later, at dawn, the crew of the *Sakhari Soiré*, helmed once again by Maguette, get into a brawl with the *Ya Fatou Ka*, a pursenetter that belongs to Djiby Dioh, the son of Joal's legendary first fisherman, Ngo Dioh. The argument nearly costs Joal its fleet.

The men will tell it so:

After a long night at sea Maguette moored the pirogue wading distance from shore in Joal's packed harbor. He had begun to haggle with the fishwives when the *Ya Fatou Ka* wedged next to the *Sakhari Soiré*. As she slid toward the shore she glanced off the starboard topside of the Souarés' pirogue, not quite scuffing it.

Hey, watch it, don't hit our boat, said Saliou, Ndongo's teenage halfbrother.

Hey, boy, don't tell me what to do, said the *Ya Fatou Ka*'s skipper.

Hey, fuck you, motherfucker, said Modou Diagne, Ndongo's maternal cousin, who is twenty-one.

Oh fuck your mother, said the man. Then two or three fishermen from the *Ya Fatou Ka* reached over and grabbed Saliou under the arms.

Accounts of what followed vary. Saliou says the men dragged him aboard their boat and someone whacked him on the back and shoulders with a loose burden board, though his only injury after the scuffle is to his right hand, knuckles bloodied as if he had punched someone or something hard. His crewmates say Saliou did get beaten up but aboard the *Sakhari Soiré*, not the other pirogue, but they are not entirely sure how that happened exactly because after the insult to his mother, Modou Diagne heaved a gasoil canister and proceeded to slosh the *Ya Fatou Ka* with fuel so he could set the pirogue on fire until someone knocked the jerrycan out of his hand and into the sea.

Picture such an exuberant conflagration! How quickly the

rush of fire licks the boat's curlicued designs and prayers off her topside and all the way to the sky. How gorgeously she burns, this mahogany pirogue caulked with tar and paint thinner—and the one not a palm's width away from her, and the next, and the next: picture, after months without a drop of rain, the holocaust of an entire seashore aflame as the fire dances from boat to boat wedged cheek by jowl above and below the tideline and loaded with fuel cans empty and full.

After the scuffle Saliou went to the harbormaster to complain about the assault and was about to head to the gendarmerie but his father forbade him from going. When I hear the story from the crew Amadou and Ndongo are at the harbor, trying to settle matters peacefully with Djiby Dioh and Harbormaster Samb. Djiby Dioh is an influential fisherman in town, and an old pal of Amadou's. Amadou does not want bad blood between him and Djiby. Besides, it is best to keep the whole arson thing from the law.

The seething crew congregate at the Souarés' compound, re-play the confrontation, scheme a retaliation with young fisher-men friends who have stopped by for gossip. It is close to noon but the fishers are unwashed, jittery from adrenaline and hunger and fatigue.

Next time I go to sea I'll bring a sword like a Fulani, wallahi, says Saliou. I won't use it, I'll just show it to them.

Next time you should go fishing with your own stick of wood, says his neighbor Modou Geye, a fisherman himself.

Next time you should get the fishermen on shore to throw

rocks at the other guys, says an *oupa* named Daouda, one of the sons of Yoro the caulker. He is fifteen but looks much younger. He is hefting a chunk of cement in his pudgy right hand.

Next time, he adds, I'll brain Amadou Souaré with a rock because he shouldn't have stopped us going to the gendarmes, wallahi.

The sea: the slow erosion of every boundary. Geography, tradition, family. Maybe this is the trouble Adama Sidy the sorcerer saw in his visions.

▽ ▵ ▽

Sundown like honey. The sea flows slow. I squeeze into the stern hold with Ousmane and Ndiaga and Vieux, dig in my drybag, and share with the boys two bananas, some candied peanuts, beignets.

You take very good care of us, Ousmane says.

I miss my son, I admit.

I am your son, he says, shines a chaplipped smile. Vieux crawls under a tarp next to me and falls asleep between the gascans and the motor.

At seven-thirty, Maguette starts the motor and lets the *Sakhari Soiré* drift alongside the net so Ndiaga Kane, El Hadj, and Cheikh Bathily can lift the net by the yellow floaters, check for catch section by section. Some sardines, not many. Maguette steers away, anchors, kills the motor. All is still again. Darkness falls heavy and the photosensor goes off in the bow and a faint red light shines from the bitt. A three-quarter moon dances in the bilges. The sea is a black pearl. It rises and falls softly in long, sweet swells. It is too quiet to talk.

Stars wheel above. Ocean wheels beneath. Before he turtles asleep inside a hooded sweatshirt Pa Diouf points a narrow finger: Polaris. He names it in Wolof: *Biddew Xibla*, the Star of Destination. Pinned to it, the world turns.

The crew doze off. In the bow Maguette boils a large pot of pearl couscous with sweet reconstituted milk for supper, covers it, ablutes for prayer. In the stern I pee into a bailing can. The second I empty it overboard, luminescence sparks up and a cricket starts in the stern. I rinse the bailing can in the twinkling ocean and laugh.

The moon goes behind some clouds. The cricket deafening, then gone. Maybe I hear the buoy of Sangomar clang once. Or maybe this is in my head. The suck and kiss of the sea against the hull: an elongated silence. Distant boats rev motors, check nets, quiet.

Quiet.

A caesura.

▽ ▵ ▽

What is it that comes next, that sudden measured breath, that almost sedate surfacing to port—two breaths, two sets of surfacings, that pass the boat from stern to bow one after the other in close and eternally slow succession and then go on and away in the dark, in the gray night, no luminescence in their wake nor at the rise and fall of their enormous streamlined hump-backed bodies? I stand and look and look. But I see nothing, and soon the coupled breath is gone.

Dolphins. Totems. Guardians.

Everyone else aboard is asleep except Maguette. The captain is praying.

▽ △ ▽

Maguette rousts the crew just before midnight. They chow down on the lukewarm pasta, shiver, pass around two hot shotglasses of sweet tea, cup the heat in their pruned fingers. The moon is out again and reflects on the sea surface in undulating stripes, white striations that make the net seem full of fish.

We haul net. The surreal phosphorous boil in its wake, its own twinkling lattice, the glossy darkness when it is finally all aboard. The men sing almost in a whisper, halfhearted from the cold. Or maybe afraid to wake something in the night. Haul like a lion—haul like a donkey—we will eat some—sardinella. Maguette and Cheikh switch on their flashlights; we pick net. Quiet shanties of other distant pirogues, other frozen, tired crews. A shooting star every time I look up. Shooting stars whenever I look away, too.

Maguette shines the flashlight at the holds, evaluates the catch by sight. No one aboard a pirogue ever says, We got a lot, or, There's too little. Fishermen appraise their haul silently and keep their judgment to themselves, and they know without discussing it what the pirogue must do next. Now the crew of the *Sakhari Soiré* know: Maguette will take this fish to Djifer, where they will spend the morning and go back out to the same fishing grounds in the afternoon. The buyers at the Djifer harbor will pay less than those in Joal but the pirogue will save on fuel.

Maguette, you sneaky bastard! You want to go to Djifer because your wife is there at her parents' house. But listen! Take care of the new baby, but don't try anything else!

Eh, what else can I try? We'll be there in daylight. I can't do anything like that in daylight.

Oh, there are plenty of things you can do in daylight.

This Maguette! He has a powerful gris-gris. He made it so the sea wouldn't have fish so he could have an excuse to play with his wife!

Guys, guys, listen, this is important. Whatever you do in Djifer, be careful where you eat. There's this one woman at the harbor, you shouldn't buy her food. I was on a boat once and we all bought lunch from her and then the whole crew had the runs. Let me tell you, there's nothing worse than a boatload full of guys who gotta go, wallahi.

True. Especially if there's only one bailing can.

That's why I always say, you've got to have at least two bailing cans.

▽ △ ▽

The net Ndongo is fixing is a purse seine half a mile long and so old it has faded from black to maroon, terracotta, beige, brown, burgundy. The job takes weeks. Ndongo spends them camped on the flat concrete roof of Khady Diallo's apartment building. He has stretched a striped white, blue, and pink tarp over the roof in lieu of a parasol; under the tarp the seine spills its soft pleats like a giant man-o-war.

A midmorning in February. A full moon pales in bright sky. In her kitchen downstairs Khady is preparing lunch on a propane burner, her makeup perfect and baby Ndeye Khady strapped to her back. She is singing under her breath along with the radio. Upstairs I shuck off my sandals, curl up in the soft shapelessness of the net, its fishy embrace. Catnap any way you like here. Wind flaps the tarp, twangs Khady's clotheslines, rushes old plastic bags through the sandy alley below and lifts them up and blows them into the net, against Ndongo's bent back, against my bare arms. The steam of Khady's *ceebu jën* winds up two concrete flights of stairs.

Ndongo, spreadlegged on the edge of the seine, stitches the floatline onto the net with blue fishing twine, counts out the stitches. Five stitches to tie the net to the line. Ten stitches to circumvent each yellow styrofoam float. Then five stitches on the line again.

Two more weeks and I'll be done, inshallah, he says.

That's a lot of lay time, I say.

You're right. But the sea will never finish. It will be there. So I have time. When I'm done with this we'll go back to the Gambia.

Vieux Sene arrives, in white earbuds and a tartan cap and a black down vest. Ndongo shows him the floatline he has been stitching on, explains his method.

What do you think?

Looks good, says Vieux. He has been hustling, mending net, selling fish, helping friends when he can. He takes off his sneakers to step onto the net, threads a shuttle with more blue twine, for Ndongo. His socks smell rotten.

And how's your own pirogue, Vieux?

Eh, it's still broken. I still don't have enough money to repair it. Soon, inshallah.

Inshallah.

An hour before lunch the net's owner arrives, removes his flip-flops, crawls up onto the summit of the net. He is a young man and last week his only wife died in childbirth; the baby lived. Now the baby is with a sister-in-law who is nursing a newborn of her own, the two older children are with the grandparents, and he is here, on Khady Diallo's roof, in the middle of his old net. Where else? I offer my condolences. Thank you. Life is so, he says. Everything is God's will.

We sit in the wind, in the blowing sand and trash. Ndongo counts out the stitches. Vieux unspools and respools blue twine, talks to someone on the phone. I take notes.

Anna, says the net owner. Will you remember all this?

I hope so. That's why I have this notebook. So that later when I look at my notes I can see everything: Ndongo and Vieux, this flapping tarp, you in the middle of the net, the smell of Khady's good food—

All the dirty plastic bags flying around—

Yes, I will remember those too.

▽ ▲ ▽

Anna. Come tomorrow. Six-forty in the morning. I want to try something different.

Ndongo plans to leave for the Gambia the next afternoon and remain there until the night-fishing season ends in May. But he wants to squeeze in a day trip off the Petite Côte before he leaves, even though there are few fish here and this is not the season for day fishing. Ndongo wants to squeeze every last fish out of the sea.

I arrive at Mbaar Kanené before first light. The world at this hour lacks definition, a flat discus smothered between low tide and a three-quarter moon. Gillnets are just arriving in Joal harbor marina, anchoring offshore to wait for the fishwives and middlemen to wake. You can see the still patch of water before the harbor flicker like a fire show with their bowlights and their burning braziers doubled in shallow reflection. Downcoast the moored pirogues, mostly jiggers, point out to sea, strain their improvised bollards: other boats, a palm trunk that rests on the sand, pirogue fragments. It is a week past spring equinox and with the first hint of light fog begins to curdle in the savannah. It will migrate to sea by noon, momentarily drowning all in milk. Then it will be burned apart and carried back eastward in tissue-thin wisps.

At ten to seven the eastern sky blushes, pales, illuminates a handful of early seagulls, the procession of pirogues strung along the horizon toward port. Illuminates the new odd seaweed the sea deposits ashore this time of the year: soft dark green tubular antlers, coral-like white constellations of white sequins. Illuminates, south of Mbaar Kanené, a purse seiner unloading her catch onto a horsecart: her captain would rather pay the cart driver than the annual harbor dues that would allow him to sell at the marina. Past this scofflaw horsecarts caravan toward the harbor. Fishwives with buckets, purposeful men. A big black sow wanders along the wrackline also, snout to the ground, her droopy teats swaying low. Above all this, on the southernmost leg of their migration, kites soar. No sign of Ndongo or his crew.

I am drinking café Touba in Mariama Boye's breakfast shack when he calls. The trip is off. Sokhna, his and Khady's daughter, is sick: unable to hold down any food, feverish. Ndongo has taken her to the Joal hospital, Khady has taken her to a convent just north of town. The nuns gave her syrup, the doctors two injections. Khady herself boiled the root of Sodom's apple and papaya leaves into a tincture. Nothing worked. Now they are taking her to a Serer village of millet farmers a few miles inland to see a local medicine woman, a sorceress. I should come too.

Dawn finds Ndongo and Khady Diallo sitting side by side on the sorceress's waiting porch, next to a hundred-pound bag of yellow onions: he on a plastic woven mat nuzzling baby Ndeye Khady's faint curls; she in a metal chair. Sokhna, in a matching wax print skirt and top over pink fleece Pokémon pajama bottoms, is draped over Khady's knees. The sick girl is weeping from pain. The night before, when Khady was nursing the baby and Sokhna had nodded off at last into restless sleep, Khady saw the disembodied head of a horse float through their room. She thinks it was the devil.

There are other patients on the porch, two women with toddlers. A teenage girl brings us some plastic cups on a dinted tin plate, a large pot of weak sweet coffee, another tin plate with halved fresh baguettes, and a message from the healer: If her medicine doesn't help, at least her patients won't go away hungry.

Ndongo tells a story:

I have this relative in the Gambia. One time he was eating and something got stuck in his throat. They took him to the local hospital but the doctors there couldn't do anything. I think this was in the port of Bakau. So they rushed him to the capital. He could barely breathe by then. The doctors in the capital were getting ready to operate on his throat, cut it open. Then one of his relatives said, Wait, before you do that let me call my friend. This friend, he was a healer, a sorcerer. He poured water into a cup, said a prayer. They lifted up the man—he was so sick by then he couldn't sit up on his own—and poured this water into his mouth. And—*wkakh*! The man spat it out. It was a fish bone.

La illaha illa Allah! say the women with the toddlers.

That's true, says Ndongo. If people in the West were like us here in Africa they wouldn't spend all the money on doctors. They would just go to a marabout or a healer in the bush.

And Khady Diallo says:

I wonder how much this medicine woman charges.

We sip the healer's coffee. A duck and a single yellow duckling parade across a large swept sun-cobbled yard, past a big mango tree with round shade and large green fruit, waddle around a tall papaya tree and disappear behind the sorceress's hut: a single rectangular cinderblock room roofed with palm thatch. The fronds of the thatch are gathered into a peak at the top and cinched with a car tire. Under an awning held by three neat wooden posts the corrugated tin door is ajar and a beige curtain billows and falls behind it like a luffing sail.

Each appointment lasts about an hour; Sokhna is third in line. At eleven in the morning Ndongo and his family enter the crepuscule of the medicine hut.

From the rafters hang strings of onions, bunches of herbs, deflated balloons of baobab fruit, a ram's horn. On the walls portraits framed and unframed: a wrestler, a man in robes, imams. On the floor a battery of plastic bottles of different sizes filled with liquid of all shades of brown and green, several baguettes wrapped in newspaper, grocery bags with something inside. Part kitchen, part shrine. On a wide bed opposite the door a young man is lying on his back. The sorceress herself sits facing the bed on a mat covered with a stained bedsheet in white and blue stripes. Her name is Khady Gning; she goes by Mère Khady. A stern-looking obese woman past her middle years. Toe rings of silver and copper on her left foot, silver rings on her left hand, copper and silver bangles on her right wrist. Her black-and-white calico dress shows a black sports bra through the armholes, her yellow homespun pagne is held in place by a red rope that dangles with many keys. I wonder whether the keys are gris-gris or to open something. Gris-gris, arguably, are to open something.

The sorceress motions for Sokhna to come close, arranges the whimpering girl between her heavy thighs, facing away, toward the bed. Ndongo sits at the foot of the mat, Khady and the baby in a chair across the hut. The sorceress spits a few times on a kerchief, takes off the girl's blouse and undoes the ties of her skirt. She spits on her fingertips now and whispers something, pats the girl gently on the shoulders and on the back. Spits and pats again. Spits faster and pats, spits and pats, spits and pats Sokhna's arms and sides and rubs the girl's forehead and temples and her orderly cornrows, faster still, as if stamping the child with many benedictions, then slows down and stops spitting and draws her left forefinger down Sokhna's nodulated spine, and, reaching the middle of the back, nods. The girl no longer whimpers. She looks stupefied. Her skirt has fallen around her and she sits with her legs splayed in those pink Pokèmon pajamas.

Breathe.

Sokhna inhales.

With the dull end of a ram's horn wrapped in green cloth Mère Khady pounds something in a calabash, then places the horn against Sokhna's back, then against her chest, dull side to skin, like a stethoscope. Against the girl's shoulder blade. Armpit. Lower back. Clavicle. Blows on the horn: now it is a shofar. The young man on the bed sits up and begins to pick his nose.

Mère Khady puts down the horn and looks up. Her inhales and exhales laborious, exasperated.

Why is this girl here?

She has a stomachache.

At this the sorceress laughs deeply, hugely.

This? This is no stomachache! This looks like evil wind to me. This looks to me like Satan.

She reaches for a plastic bottle of pale-brown liquid, gives it to Ndongo, helps the girl on her feet.

Bathe her with this.

▽ ▲ ▽

When Ndongo and Sokhna return from the washroom the girl slips lightly into Mère Khady's vast embrace. She has perked up. She plays with the ties of her skirt, looks around, studies the dried plants that hang from the rafters. The medicine woman pats dry her bare shoulders with a rag and speaks to her parents.

You have to take care of your children. You can't tell small children not to run around in the street, but you can protect them. Trust me, I'm Muslim, I won't lie to you. This one, it seems that her soul doesn't work very well. I think you have no protection in your house. So you are letting people cast an evil eye on her.

She points at Khady Diallo.

Especially you. It's a woman's job to make sure her children are safe. And your husband wasted his time today. If it weren't for this he would have gone to sea. Instead, he had to come here.

You're right, we don't have any gris-gris at home, Khady says.

That's a mistake. You don't give her herbal baths, you don't have any gris-gris for her—

She presses Sokhna's stomach lightly.

Does this hurt? No? Okay, God willing when you take the medicine I give you, you will feel better.

The sorceress gives Khady Diallo a length of thin brown rope with many knots to wrap around Sokhna's waist and instructs that the girl wear it always. She gives her two bottles of opaque liquid: one dark like coffee, the other pale with green flecks. On the first day Khady must mix a spoonful of the dark liquid with water, salt, sugar, and a whole baobab fruit, bring everything to a boil, take out the baobab seed, and have Sokhna drink the brew. On the second day she must substitute baobab fruit with tea. She must add the other liquid to Sokhna's bathwater for three days straight. On the fourth day, she must bring Sokhna back for a checkup.

Thank you, Mère Khady. How much?

Give me what your heart tells you to give me. And when you return bring me four yards of any kind of fabric. What's your name, child?

Sokhna.

The woman laughs her big laugh again.

Okay, Sokhna. When you grow up and have a husband you will give me this very pretty dress you're wearing.

The sorceress stops me as we are filing out the door.

I see you are writing things down. Write this: I am a very famous healer. Sometimes I make forty bottles of this potion and send it to France, to Spain, to Switzerland. People all over the world know me! At the airport in Dakar, people step off the plane and the first thing they ask the gendarmes is, Do you know Mère Khady?

It is an honor to meet you, madame. Thank you for helping my friends' daughter. If I get sick and I can't figure out how to treat it I will come to you.

The woman looks me in the eye. Then she laughs again.

You won't get sick.

On the way out we pass two dozen men and women and a few children waiting in the blue shadow of the mango tree. More patients wait on the porch. Some will spend the night here to have their appointment with the sorceress.

We were lucky we didn't have to wait very long, says Khady Diallo. And Ndongo says:

Next time I return from the sea I will come back to see this woman by myself. I need some good fishing gris-gris.

▽ △ ▽

'm not surprised, says Fatou Diop Diagne when I mention Sokhna's illness and the trip to the sorceress. A few days ago that girl came here and she had an abscess on her head, so it became quite clear that Khady doesn't take care of her.

We are in Fatou's spacious sitting room. She is entertaining Amadou's new fourth wife from Kaolak, a voluptuous woman in careful makeup and many gold bangles who is visiting for a few days. She is sitting on a couch and flipping through television channels with a remote. An Indian soap opera. Hip-hop videos. A laamb wrestling match. Fatou says:

I don't understand what kind of a person this Khady Diallo is. She doesn't talk to any of us. Her upbringing seems to be no good at all.

Mm-hmm. Girl has no manners, the wife from Kaolak says without looking away from the screen, which she has tuned to a talk show about matrimonial jealousy.

And Fatou says:

I don't know this healer personally but I've heard about her. And I'll tell you something, Anna, my friend. I can't rule out that because of the discord between Khady and our family, our family genii became upset.

▽ ▲ ▽

You don't go to sea if someone is sick at home, fishermen say. In a taxi from Mère Khady's, Ndongo says he will postpone the Gambia tour. But he is obsessed. Two hours later my phone rings. The *Sakhari Soiré* sails in an hour. Ndongo wants me to come to see him off, say goodbye. Also, if I no longer need my drybag, he really could use it.

Last hours ashore, those hours before the insatiable charge of the hunt, are a slough: there is still time. Boys and men board pirogues slowly, as if in a daze. They check flashlight batteries, buy baggies of dry dates, of peanuts, buy extra cellphone credit. They call their girlfriends, lovers, wives. They hold in their hands their flipflops, fuel lines, cellphones, rubberized overalls, provisions wrapped in newspaper or plastic. They do not talk to one another much. They do not smile, these penitents. They watch the sea, toe the surf's soft fluttering lip. Generations straddle this unsubstantiated faultline, this entry point to the mysterious and vast waterworld, the site of many rites of passage, a point of departure and a port of return.

▽ ▲ ▽

Hot sticky sun. Tide coming in. Terrycloth clouds on the horizon. Three little *oupa* boys squat just above the surfline. They are building two sandcastles.

These are mosques, says one.

No, these are palaces, says another.

Whose palaces are these? I ask.

This one belongs to the president of Senegal.

No, this one is Yékini's!

And this other one is Balla Gaye's!

They are beautiful.

You like them?

Yes, very much.

Look, look at this one. This one is for Eumeu Sène!

Twenty minutes later nothing remains of the sandcastles and the boys are lugging five-gallon jerrycans with water and fuel aboard three different pirogues, getting ready to cast off, heading to sea.

▽ △ ▽

Ndongo is waiting for me on a midship thwart of a beached nine-foot trapsetter. He is wearing gray sweatpants and a flamingo-pink tee shirt, a sweatshirt, a sweater tied crosswise on his chest, blue flipflops on bare feet. He is swinging his legs. Little Sokhna is really feeling much better, he says. She will be fine, inshallah. Did you bring your drybag?

The *Sakhari Soiré*'s complement assembles on the shore. Boys will crew the boat on this trip: Ousmane, Ousmane's friend Ndiaga Kane, Ndongo's nephew Ibrahima, five other teenagers. Captain Ndongo will be the only adult aboard.

Ousmane, lips purulent and awful, in blue shorts and a striped gray sweater several sizes too small, is pushing the boat off to sea from the shallows alone. Seagulls shriek.

Well.

Well.

Ndongo and I shake left hands, to warrant fair winds and following seas, to ensure that we meet again in this life. A fisherman's life, like an itinerant storyteller's, brims with goodbyes. I watch him and his boys wade aboard the *Sakhari Soiré*, watch a horsecart back up into the sea and unload the pirogue's outboard and a spare. I have an impulse to wade in, too, and climb aboard the pirogue one last time and set out even for just a few breaths and then jump off her stern inscribed with my name, splash to shore in dripping skirts. But it would make no difference, cross no real lines, realign no boundaries. It would become a story men eventually would tell at the *mbaar*, like everything else.

▽ ▲ ▽

Late afternoon ashore, spring, an hour to high tide. The sun almost directly overhead, boat shadows sharp and short. The sea a boundless incandescence.

Watch the sea form and reform with each heave, rearrange itself into a sea deceptively new though nothing moving on Earth is older. A traceless wholeness that seems unadulterated, sealed upon itself no matter how much you take out of it, abundant in plentitude and paucity, awash in memory and promise.

A group of men lounge inside a *mbaar*, flat silhouettes against the glare. One walks off, kneels by the wrackline facing the water. Why? Why not? I would be praying, too. In a way, I am. The man stands up and turns around and walks back toward his friends, still zipping up his fly. On the ocean, each of us is a mystic and a jester, and nothing ever is what we imagine it to be.

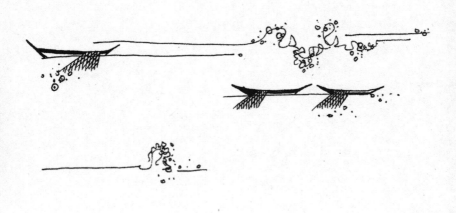

Acknowledgments

The generosity and candor of my captains, hosts, and fellow voyagers in Senegal and across the world made possible my research. A casita on a friend's ranch in the northern Chihuahuan Desert, at the bottom of an ancient sea, made possible the quiet solitude of writing.

Conversations with my parents, my sister, and my son, Fyodor; sessions with my counselor; and the rise and pitch of my most intimate friendships helped shape and reshape my thoughts about boundaries. Verónica, Thorne, Shenid, Sally, Nicol, Mattie, Lori, Kael, Jim, Gözde, Dominic, Carlos, Basil, Azza.

Boris Boubacar Diop, Dominic Duval-Diop, Gaoussou Gueye, El Hadji Faye, Bob Jones, Krista Larson, Jori Lewis, Gabi Matthews, and Abdou Karim Sall offered indispensable oceanic advice. My comrades Ben Fountain and David Searcy were early listeners. Thank you, Geri Thoma, for the necessary life preservers.

Charles Digges, my first reader always, and Becky Saletan, Katie Freeman, Michelle Koufopoulos, Anna Jardine, Maureen Klier, and the rest of the Riverhead crew: your magnanimous attention honors my work.

Every word in this book is a word of gratitude.